The Birth of the Lion

Non-Duality as a Way of Life

by OM C. Parkin

Consciousness Classics
Gateways Books and Tapes
Nevada City, California
2016

ISBN 978-0-89556-276-0
First Gateways Books edition

Text © 2016 by OM C. Parkin

Original Edition from Advaita Media, Germany:
The Birth of the Lion: Dialogues of Self-Inquiry
Translated from the German original by Anama Frühling
ISBN: 3-936718-02-4 (hardcover)
Cover Design by Gailyn Bering-Porter
All Rights Reserved
Published by Gateways Books and Tapes
IDHHB, Inc.
PO Box 370
Nevada City, CA 95959
USA
Phone: (800) 869-0658 or (530) 271-2239
E-mail: info@gatewaysbooksandtapes.com
Website: http://www.gatewaysbooksandtapes.com

Library of Congress CIP Data

Table of Contents

iii

FOREWORD

"Out of ignorance this universe seems to appear in many forms, but in reality all of these are Brahman—that which remains when all states of mind have been renounced. Everything that is believed to be separate from Brahman has no grounds for being. The highest Brahman is the only reality without any other. There is only one, not two. It is pure wisdom, flawless, perfect peace without any doing, without beginning and without end. Its nature is unending bliss. When all differences created by Maya (illusion) have been rejected, there remains something that shines by itself that is eternal, flawless, immeasurable, and indestructible. The sages recognize it as the highest truth, the absolute consciousness in which the one that realizes, the realized, and realizing are united, unending, and unchanging.

"Give up the idea of a 'me' with family, relatives, name, character, and position in life, all of which depend on this physical body. Become the essential form that is absolute Bliss, after having also dropped the qualities of the ethereal body, as well as the feeling of being the doer. It is only after the complete disappearance of the 'I-thought,' and the destruction of all its deceptive demonstrations, that the essential truth of 'I am That' is revealed by the discrimination between the false self and the true Self."

The Jewel of Discrimination
Shankara (788 – 820 A.D.)

As someone in love with the pearls of realization found in literary scriptures of wisdom, I could go on quoting from these texts in endless enthusiasm. Through these verses, the nature of enlightenment is somehow clearly expressed in spite of limited linguistic means, in spite of translation, and in spite of a gap of more than a thousand years!

In the past twenty-five years, I have had the great good luck of meeting in form with such "authorities of the absolute." For instance, the meeting with Anandamayi Ma was and is for me living proof of how divine realization can reveal it*Self* even today. After having followed for many years the traditional transmission of Bhakti (the loving devotion to a chosen ideal), the path of Jnana, or realization and Self-inquiry, has also gained importance for me in recent years. Both the teachings of Shri Ramana Maharshi and Nisargadatta Maharaj have transmitted deep insights into the immortal inner being and above all, have not erected new limits as can come into existence all too easily by becoming a follower of certain paths and traditions. Perhaps it was their naked clarity and the ruthlessness of their inquiry, the rather male polarity of realization that I had been awaiting.

In 1996, an acquaintance told me about a German man who had experienced awakening to his true Self after a car accident. I came across a booklet entitled *The Myth of Enlightenment.*[*] I started to read it in passing, initially with the attitude of, "Aha, one more of these so-called enlightened persons. . . ." Until relatively recently, the historically credible enlightened ones were mostly established in India and here in the West were not exactly

---

[*] Om C. Parkin, *The Myth of Enlightenment: An Interview with Om C. Parkin*, Hamburg: Satsang Allionce, 1996.

encountered in large numbers. Because of this, such a claim of enlightenment just had to be viewed critically at first.

When I read the booklet, however, these considerations soon faded into the background. My heart started pounding and a feeling of inner acceleration occurred, as if all my ready-made constructions of "That is me and that is the world" collapsed like a house of cards. A "Fall into the Bottomless" took place in which I was deprived of all supports, and the illusory character of "Chandravali and her world" was revealed. What I had read about "pure consciousness" in the scriptures was suddenly no longer theoretical.

Did this experience have something to do with OM C. Parkin whom I had just read an interview about? Did "I" have something to do with "him"? Rather than the usual perception of "me" and "other," my inner experience was more like a partaking of that same background that is always present like a screen, normally overshadowed by the flickering dramas of our lives, but which doesn't belong to anyone "personally." Regardless, some weeks later I attended a "Darshan" with OM, but compared to the inner experience, the physical encounter was not decisive. Rather, perhaps, it served to connect "tools," in this case the editor, author, and publisher of the book you are now reading.

Shortly before Christmas, there was a call from OM, inquiring if I could imagine putting a book together from the transcriptions of recorded Darshans that had taken place until that time. I was enthusiastic, as this meant both work and a deepening of spiritual recognition at the same time. When I got the first fifty pages from OM, a strange feeling of dizziness would occur at times as if I was entering an empty space.

The approximately 500 pages of transcribed material originated from Darshans held with OM between

December 1994 and March 1997, as well as from interviews with the journalist and author Christian Salvesen pertaining to particular subjects. In Darshan, OM accompanies the seeker in his or her own process of inquiry, meeting each person exactly where they are in their own individual process. The interviews deal with important questions of a philosophical nature. The different parts of the material came together according to an inner law, as if growing organically like a plant. Repetition and overlapping could not always be avoided in order to retain coherence. The meaningfulness and authenticity of the material affected me deeply. These pages are evidence of individual awakening, as well as a precise guide to Self-inquiry coupled with a Western psychologist's incorruptible understanding of the false, limiting structures of ego.

The teaching of Advaita, or non-duality, did not run dry after Ramana Maharshi, nor did it remain in India. Inexorably, its silent power goes on radiating in the West, inviting us all to Satsang and exposing the myth by which Western man has ensconced enlightenment as something far away from *here* and *now*.

Fellow seekers who have stayed faithful to traditional paths may remain reserved and critical, particularly as OM is not at all concerned with supporting the traditional image of a saint. One friend, however, said, "Perhaps by this God is demonstrating that enlightenment is also possible outside of tradition." How inessential and pale these notions are of "outside" and "inside," "traditional" and "untraditional" in the face of ultimate truth! Ultimately, they have no significance. The spoken words are not OM's personal message or his instructions for the world. They are an impersonal transmission of Truth, the Self, the Divine, manifesting through this form of the One Teacher. "Are you sure *I* said all of that?" OM once asked me during the week we were working together on the book. Wild geese fly across water that shows their reflections. It is neither their intention nor that of the lake to create a reflection; it just happens.

OM is the sound of the absolute, belonging to no one yet everyone may hear it. In the stillness of the heart is revealed: You *are* already what you are searching for.

Chandravali Schang
Lohmar, Germany, November 1997

Translator's Note: For this English version of *The Birth of the Lion,* the original 390 pages had to be reduced to 250 pages for editorial reasons. Although the choice was difficult, as every page without exception is an expression of Truth, I feel that the abridged version nevertheless transmits the message just as perfectly.

I am very grateful to Shanti Einolander for her brilliant editorial work on the translation, which has helped to make this book a very appropriate vehicle for the transmission.

AN AUTOBIOGRAPHY

The Search for Another Reality

When I was eighteen years old, it suddenly became very bad. From the outside, it seemed to be a typical crisis of an adolescent troubled by the fears and insecurities of passage into adult life.

Until that time, my life had been quite normal. I had experienced a sheltered childhood, as a member of a middle class family, in a very beautiful health resort on the northern Heath near Hamburg. We lived in a spacious country house with a marvelous, large garden. As the house was situated directly on the edge of a forest, we children used the forest as a big playground in which to have adventures and romp about.

I was the planned, first-born child of my parents. Naturally, great dramas of jealousy took place when my siblings were born and disputed my position. Yet, as a whole, these natural dynamics of family life were an expression of the relatively healthy family structure that supported me. The routine of everyday life — family activities, school, sports, and games — had more or less successfully covered a lack of contentment and joy. Looking back, I can say that what I had experienced was a latent depression.

I had just passed the Abitur, the final exams at High School, with little enthusiasm when suddenly a big, black hole opened up inside me for no apparent reason. Certainly, for the past several years there had been feelings of dark foreboding. I hadn't really enjoyed anything at school. I had begun experimenting with drugs and had gotten into trouble with the police. Experiences with hallucinogenic drugs had opened up my perception to realms in which I felt somehow "closer" to my origin than in my normal state of consciousness. I was starting to suspect that there was "something wrong" with the perception of everyday consciousness.

It was at this point that I first consciously met the great power of the psyche, which seemed to control and fixate perception to a certain reality. Now, the door to another reality, an *inner* reality, was opening up. What seemed cruel, however, was that access to this inner world, in all its abundance and diversity, seemed possible only while under the influence of drugs. Each time the trip was over, I was ruthlessly expelled once again from the gates of the apparent paradise. I was caught, a prisoner of my own perception.

Under these circumstances I saw only one way out. I had to learn more about the psyche. I had gained the certainty that an invisible power existed hidden behind the world, or at least what my perception would have me see as "the world." I wanted to spare no effort to find out who or what this invisible power was. The outer life, including eating, drinking, working, even juvenile pleasures, seemed to be a burden, a necessary evil. It was all a nuisance to me and seldom gave me any real joy.

Given all of this, what made more sense than to apply to study psychology at the university? I had some very good luck. Through a certain quota needed for foreigners, I got one of the greatly desired spaces of enrollment at the university of Hamburg, despite the high restrictions in numbers. To make a long story short, I was taught a lot about statistics and psychological testing, but I learned only very little about the nature of the psyche. Yet, my studies and everything around them, including my associations with other students, helped me to continue with my exploration of the psyche.

After three years, I broke off my studies due to a lack of motivation. At that time, I met my first spiritual teacher at a health fair that included psychology and esotericism. He was a Moroccan and had been trained by North-African Sufis. The Sufis have developed very refined techniques for attaining states of expanded consciousness through monotonous, rhythmic movements, breathing techniques, and the repetition of certain sounds. These states were called "trances." The possibility of attaining such states without the help of drugs appealed to me immensely. I was on a desperate search. Looking back, I have to say that I was neither conscious of what, exactly, I was searching for, nor of my desperation.

In a moment of clarity, I wrote in my diary:

"My goal is the path of salvation. The path of salvation is the path towards becoming one with God. In this life, there will be no end to the path, I am absolutely certain. The comforts and distractions are too big, the temptations too incalculable."

Only years later, after I had been separated from my teacher for a long time, did I recognize that my search for contact with the "supernatural" was actually a subconscious search for something totally different. It was a search to fulfill an unconscious lust for power. This misunderstanding would have serious consequences, which would only become apparent much later on.

The Pact

At the end of the eighties, I was working closely with a group of spiritual seekers in Austria. Once or twice a year we met for nocturnal rituals in which we accompanied each other on inner journeys. One night I had started a journey with an apparently harmless request: I wanted to learn more about the origin of my basic fear of other people and the whole world.

Suddenly, I found myself in a vaulted cellar. Underground walkways had been cut into the rock, which gleamed like copper in the light of candles attached to the walls. A festive and sublime atmosphere emanated from these walls as I moved through the long walkways and entered a large, round hall topped by a dome.

The golden gleam of the big altar candles lit the room only dimly. There reigned an absolute silence. I looked around the circle. Satan and his high priests had come together for this ritual. There stood the twelve rulers of the underworld, eleven powerful figures in black flowing robes and one in white.

I was certain of my inner guidance, and this instilled me with absolute trust. Every image and thought went by with the precision of Swiss clockwork. I had come to dissolve "the pact." I had just begun to look around when the thread of consciousness was broken and the continuity of the vision stopped. A new image appeared: I saw my soul on its journey of incarnation into the world. When I was passing through the gateway, a guard stopped me before I could leave the vault. It was an angel of perfect beauty, his blue eyes like ice. His name was Lucifer. He preferred to be called "His Majesty," though mankind

called him "the fallen angel." He introduced himself as a
messenger of God in charge of establishing the conditions
for entry into this Earth, and his job was to ensure that
those conditions were kept. He then went into a discourse
about the rapturous conditions of life on earth.

The moment we sealed our deal for my entry into
Earth, something strange happened. An enormous power
split in two and I forgot. I forgot the angel. I forgot the
deal. I forgot who *I am*. It dawned on me that this deal was
a pact. I called it the "temptation," and it started to work
mercilessly from the very moment the pact was sealed.
Again and again, this temptation re-manifested in a
thousand disguises, in unending variety, immeasurable
and greedy.

How had this happened? I had forgotten. And yet, I
recognized the pact was something like an entry ticket.
There was no soul in the whole world who had not entered
into this pact with the devil, for without this entry ticket,
no one had ever seen the theatre from the inside. Within
the theatre, the power of the guard is omnipresent, yet
everyone believes they have snuck past him, and he laughs
up his sleeve, because as long as they believe this, he has
them firmly under his control.

Once again, I consciously returned to the moment of
the pact, and then I suddenly knew that I had come
voluntarily after all. No soul is ever taken prisoner by
Lucifer.

Slowly my attention returned to the hall in which
the circle of rulers of the underworld met. I realized they
did nothing but deal with my commission and yield to my
intention. As hard and ruthless as the apprenticeship was,
everything functioned according to exactly established
laws. These were divine laws, for there are no other laws. It
was up to this illustrious circle of divine messengers to
utilize temptation to seduce souls into being human,

thereby falling into sin and separation, and thereby providing them the opportunity to recognize and remember God.

The meaning of Lucifer is "the one who brings the light." I could not help laughing. What a play, this divine play. I let my gaze wander around the circle again. These were powerful men, but their faces seemed to be careworn by the laws of the underworld, severe teachers from whose faces the joys of life had departed.

One of these men was completely different, a beautiful, charismatic adolescent, with soft, light features, dressed in white. A harp would have completed the picture perfectly. Of all people, what was this beautiful, Venus-like man doing in this circle? I received the answer: "He is the demon-angel." I could hardly believe that this man embodied the aspect of "devil" while manifesting in the form of an angel.

The scene faded into another.

Suddenly I found myself in the dining hall of a country house in the south of Spain, the residence of a lady with whom I was briefly acquainted. Sylvia, a woman in her mid forties, was known in the area as a radiant and generous hostess of opulent meals. She was soft and of a gracefulness I had know only from fairy tales about princesses. I saw only one scene, which was from the following dream she had described to me weeks ago: The last rays of the setting sun streamed through big arched windows made of blown glass, bathing the dining hall in a golden light. The spacious table, adorned with a white, silk tablecloth, was covered by royal foods. About fifteen guests had come together that evening to be lavishly entertained by Sylvia, the hostess. Sylvia, dressed in white and delicate, watercolor blue, was sitting at the end of the table engaged in a lively conversation with an elderly gentleman to her left. The stylish ambience seemed to fit harmoniously with the company at the table.

Suddenly, my gaze moved to under the table and I froze. There, Sylvia's two Afghan dogs squatted, greedily licking the blood from a sword she held under the table in her right hand, their craving tongues stretched out. Once again the words "demon-angel" appeared in my consciousness. Shocked, my inner attention shifted back to the catacombs in which I had visited, back to the pretty boy in the circle of the twelve. There, I finally understood Mephisto in Goethe's "Faust," who announces, "I am part of the force that only wants to do evil and yet always creates good." Thus, I perceived him as a power beyond the forms of good and evil. He could take possession of any form he chose. In other words, he was capable of appearing in every form of this world. The concepts that Christianity, in particular the Church, held about the devil were revealed to be mere shadow projections of the animal forces that man had himself split off from. My inner guidance cautioned me to remember my mission.

Looking around in the circle, I knew at once who my party was in the pact. When I stepped forward to face him, I saw him smile for the first time, and I was touched by the friendliness his features expressed. His name was Orwhan.

I heard myself say, "I have come to dissolve the pact. The time has come. I have been serving for a long time, and I have learned a lot."

Only the gift of recognizing and remembering the tenets of the pact had made this moment possible. I wondered what I had sold for this pact and what I had received.

Orwhan had revealed to me, "The quality of a warm, compassionate heart is unnecessary, even a hindrance, on the path toward power." He had been trying to tempt me with knowledge, an instrument created solely for accumulating more and more power, the power of rule and domination over others. "What you get back," he said, "is your heart, for only those who have recognized the pact return here, and believe me, they are few. It is the pact around which the whole earthly drama revolves. The only reason for entering into it in the first place is to recognize it, break it up, and thus remember what is beyond the pact. But if you believe that the pact will have lost its effect in the next moment, you are mistaken. Remember the laws of time and space on this earth. Matter is inert and the pact lingers within you. The sacrifice of the ego that has to be made is immense. Consequently, the trials, which will only begin now, will be immense. Only they will show whether your decision is really the final decision. Go now and use what you have learned here in service of the One."

Bits and pieces of thoughts passed through my consciousness. Everything started vibrating within me, at first very subtly, and soon more and more strongly. Again and again, I asked myself, "How long have you waited for this moment?" Joy spread through me, an inner dancing and rejoicing, a lightness. It was as if an immense burden had been lifted and vanished.

"The devil is evil; God is good," said the devil, and the firmament trembled as he burst into reverberating laughter, and all the angels and demons joined in.

The Romanticism of Death

—July 1990, Vorarlberg, Austria, in a mountain hut.

It was deadly quiet in the room. The effect of the drug suddenly began with certain physical sensations I was quite familiar with. In the course of my experiments with hallucinogenic drugs, I had learned that only very few of the hallucinations occurring on every level of perception contained essential information. Most of them offered extremely pleasurable experiences, it was true, but those distracted from the potential for self-recognition made accessible by the drug. I considered them to be "side effects," similar to the side effects of orthodox medicines. Most drug consumers, however, took hallucinogenic drugs precisely to enjoy these embellishments and to "get high." It was as if God had placed a web of distractions in front of this powerful instrument of recognition in which every user is first checked by the integrity of his or her intentions.

I paid no attention to the strong sensory impressions setting in. Suddenly, from a deeper level, a crystal clear image, complete with an impressive blaze of colors, appeared as if on a large-scale video display. Immediately I started to describe it to my companion. The image revealed a large plain, a prairie landscape like in the southwestern United States. The entire plain was covered with dead bodies. The battle was over. No one was alive, and there was no vegetation, so my gaze could wander freely across the large plains to a chain of mountains lining the distant horizon.

On the right side of the picture, large in the foreground, there seemed to be a survivor. Someone was sitting on a horse. It was a skeleton with a banner in its right hand raised in triumph. I had never consciously met this figure before, and even in this moment, I didn't recognize it as an obvious personification of death. The sun, a huge semicircle of fire, was setting behind the mountains and bathed the entire plains in a deeply orange light. A weird silence weighed on everything. Nothing lived. Yet, the silence didn't feel threatening to me. On the contrary, even the cruelly injured bodies radiated deep peace.

The whole picture exerted such a strong pull, I felt as if I were being sucked into it. Without any interpretation, I *purely* perceived this force as well. My description was naive and innocent, for I had no access to analytical thought. I expressed to my companion directly and simply what I perceived.

After I had finished my description, I asked him what it all meant. He was quiet for a moment, and then dryly commented that apparently some kind of longing for death was expressing itself through my vision. This meant nothing to me. I couldn't relate his comment to my life. I was still totally absorbed in the picture when suddenly a thought appeared, unveiled and crystal clear:

"The Romanticism of Death"

Apparently, this was the title of the image I had seen. I was not even surprised. There was just an inner shrug . . . a lack of understanding. I didn't know what to do with this title, so for the time being my experience ended in a lack of understanding.

* * *

Only a few weeks later, just after midnight on August 6, 1990, I got into my car in Hamburg to drive to my residence in the northern Lüneburg Heath.

Suddenly, there was a deafening crack — and the film of my life events came to a dead stop.

Newspaper Article: Speeding Driver Seriously Injured

"Harmstorf — Twenty-seven-year-old Cedric P. was seriously injured in a car accident on Country Road 214 close to the village of Harmstorf. Apparently, he had been driving too fast. On a slight, right-hand curve of the wet road entering the village of Harmstorf, he lost control over his dark-blue Mercedes station wagon. The car went into a skid and crashed head-on into a tree, where he was pinned in the wreckage of his car. Firemen from Harmstorf and Bendestorf, as well as paramedics, cut the seriously injured man out of the car, and he was later treated by emergency doctors."

"The Mercedes station wagon was completely smashed in the accident. The driver was quite lucky under the circumstances. He was seriously injured, but he survived."

Gegen Baum geprallt

nm. HARMSTORF. Schwerer Unfall am Ortseingang Harmstorf: Ein aus Richtung Helmstorf auf der Landstraße 213 fahrender Mercedes-Kombi kam aus bisher ungeklärter Ursache von der Fahrbahn ab und prallte gegen einen Baum. Der 28jährige Fahrer, Cedric P., wurde lebensgefährlich verletzt in seinem Wagen eingeklemmt, mußte von Blauröcken der Feuerwehren Harmstorf und Bendestorf aus dem Unfall-Wrack befreit werden. Anschließend wurde der Verletzte mit Notarzt und Rettungswagen in das Buchholzer Krankenhaus gebracht. Foto: nh

The Beginning of the End of a Dream

The first visual impressions and sensations slowly formed a new picture—a bed, a body, intravenous tubes, a hospital. The moment of awakening was the resumption of the film, but now there seemed to be no one who awoke, no "me." Slowly, from the accrued perceptions of many moments, a body reconstructed in consciousness. A person took shape. This person, however, was not "me." It was just another object in my perception. It was a shock to realize that without any doubt "I" totally existed, yet the body didn't exist, nor even the world. I was immortal! It was inconceivable. By the grace of God I was allowed to experience an interruption in the stream of perceptions. The dimension of time and space had disappeared, and even the original dualism between the experiencer and the experienced had ceased to exist.

For two days, I had been clinically dead. For unknown reasons, only a few minutes from my destination, without applying any brakes, I had driven my car off the road and crashed head-on into a hundred-year-old oak at fifty miles per hour. It was only due to several lucky coincidences that the body had the chance to survive at all. That the body could be welded out of the car and rescued only a short time after the accident could even be called a miracle.

My existence as an individual had been shattered, and I was unable to share my experience with other people. Physically and emotionally, the whole organism seemed to be in a kind of stupor. I experienced total indifference towards what I had until then considered as "life." Life suddenly appeared to be a stream of empty, insignificant phenomena arising from *that which I am*—eternal consciousness.

As I was awakening from the coma, a friend standing by my bedside asked me what I had experienced. I could not help thinking of all the reports of so-called near death experiences. I had read reports of out of the body experiences in books by Elisabeth KüblerRoss, and I had also read about long, dark tunnels at the end of which a shining light appeared. When descriptions came to mind of being kidnapped by aliens, I smiled. What had *I* experienced? Nothing of the kind.

I had experienced *nothing*. Yet even this expression does not come close to the experience itself, for *nothing* is not "nothing." To describe this nothing, I would need to go beyond the limits of language as a fundamentally dualistic instrument. There had been no "I" to experience anything, for that would signify a separation between the subject and the object of perception. The "waves" of perception had abruptly quieted down, and "I" was an ocean of limitless consciousness without any form and without any qualities. It was the pure *I am*. In an indescribable way this ocean was conscious of itself, even though there was nobody and nothing aware of the ocean.

After reawakening, a creeping process of re-identification with I-thoughts set in, yet oceanic consciousness still penetrated the entirety of perception. I experienced the body as an empty shell, without significance, and no longer necessary for the existence and completeness of my *Self*. Everything that had been "reality" suddenly appeared empty and without meaning.

My family and old friends came to see me in the hospital, but I was unable to communicate with them. Neither was I much interested, because they could not truly *see* me. They believed I still suffered from narcotics and from the shock of the accident. Apart from that, I seemed totally "normal" to them.

The healing process of the body progressed very rapidly. It seemed at first that except for a trauma to the skull and the brain, some broken ribs and bad bruises, I had not contracted any serious injuries.

In just a few days after awakening from the coma, I was up on my feet again. One evening I was sitting outside on the balcony adjoining my room, when I felt a sudden urge to call a friend in Vienna. He was the organizer of a therapeutic training I had started the year before. The second part of this training was to take place the following week at a castle in the mountains near Vienna. On the phone I told my friend what had happened, and that in spite of my condition, I felt the urge to travel to Austria. I knew that it was impossible for me to assist with the training, but I felt it was essential for me to be there with my group. At first he considered this intention crazy and agreed with my doctors who thought the journey absolutely irresponsible at that time. But I would not be argued out of my desire, and taking full responsibility for any danger, I traveled to Vienna by train in a compartment for the disabled.

When I reached the castle of Plankenstein where the training was taking place, I understood the reason for my journey. Gangaji, the wife of my trainer, Eli Jaxon-Bear, had come with him to Austria and was holding *Satsang** in the evenings. Gangaji had realized enlightenment with an Indian master, and he had given her the task of going "door to door" to share her experience.

I had not yet been drawn to Eastern religions or read any books by Indian masters. But despite that, or perhaps because of it, it felt totally natural for me to be in Satsang

---

* Indicates words whose definition can be found in the glossary at the back of the book.

with Gangaji. It was as if I had always been in Satsang with her.

Immediately in the first Satsang, I recognized her as my final teacher. By everything she said and everything she did not say, she pointed me to the direct experience of my immortal Self. I could not have been more open to hear this message than at this time when the whole identification with my personality had collapsed like a house of cards. A close connection with Gangaji developed, which I expressed in my letters to her.

The following two months I spent in a state characterized by carelessness and indifference. I neither felt any direct connection to the body nor experienced emotions of any kind. In Hamburg, I sometimes went for a walk in the streets and imagined someone stabbing my body with a knife. I found that I was completely indifferent to death. I lived in the recognition that death exists only as a concept, not as a reality.

I was not in any shape to attend a daily job. However well my "gross" wounds and injuries from the accident were healing, it soon became clear that the central nervous system had been deeply traumatized as well. The selective process of the millions of stimulating impulses rushing into the brain each moment, particularly through the eyes and ears, no longer seemed to function properly. Thus, there was a total "overload" as soon as the number of stimuli reached a certain level. It was impossible for me to stay at a café or restaurant, and even shopping in the supermarket became torture. Headaches, raised eye pressure, a stiff neck, and severe weakness were only some of the symptoms.

I remember exactly the rainy November day in 1990 when, while sitting at my desk, it became clear that I had to start taking care of my finances again. A wave of fear arose with thoughts about my empty bank account and obligations to current expenses.

The fear took me by surprise. I had felt no emotion since the accident. But now fear was a very different experience than it had been in the past. It was pure and not accompanied by thought. The intensity of the feeling grew stronger and stronger, becoming more intense than I had ever known. At a certain point, there was an impulse to go crazy and run out into the street. The thought arose, "This must be paranoia." At the same time, I was sitting there in complete stillness, a silent witness to what was happening. I witnessed the wave of fear, and for the first time did not interfere. Nobody did anything. I could watch the astonishing spectacle of fear swelling into a gigantic, threatening wave just to sink back into nothingness. Minutes later, the experience was over.

I was deeply impressed that the power and intensity of this negative feeling did not seem to touch me, the Self. From that time on, states of fear occurred every day, without warning, and not related to any thoughts. Later, I understood through Gangaji that as the thoughts calm down and the mind surrenders to stillness, all of the suppressed subconscious material of the past rises up into consciousness to be burned away. That same month I received this letter from Gangaji:

"I know it must be a strong experience to leave the material world behind, because now you see the lie much more clearly. You said that since the accident you have a feeling of no longer being part of this life. That is the truth! You are life. Explore who you really are by discovering what never changes."

It was true that I'd had a penetrating experience of oneness beyond all phenomena, but I felt I had not yet completely realized the actual core of suffering. On a subtle level, in both conscious and unconscious thoughts, the identification with the person, at that time called "Dervish," had begun to build once again. I still experienced separation.

Nothing in my life held importance any longer. Gangaji was the only person to whom I could open. One single desire started to completely take possession of me, and that was for liberation from the inherent human state of separation from divine Self, from the Source.

Things that had once been important, such as social contacts with friends, suddenly meant nothing. I started to withdraw more and more. I experienced other people, including some of my old friends, as living in a kind of sleepwalking state. I saw that they did not really communicate with each other, but instead communicated with self-created images from the past, which they then projected onto the other person. Nobody really communicated with me *now*. Therefore, I disengaged from old "relationships." My need for external seclusion supported an inner process, a process that I experienced as a progressive detachment from the illusion that the human mind calls "the world." It was as if the waters of the ocean were carrying me, and I was slowly sinking deeper into it.

Nothing could be done to accelerate this sinking into the ocean. Rather, there needed to be a rejection of all habitual ways of thinking, feeling, and acting that created the tendency for "me" to resurface again and again. It was crushing to have to see that the whole of my conditioned thinking, all of my attempts to reach happiness on earth through understanding, knowledge, and security, directly created the opposite; that is to say, suffering.

For the first time, I understood the mechanics of suffering in all its dimensions. It was so obvious. How on earth could it have been hidden? How was it possible that I had never been completely aware of this suffering, and therefore, never had the desire to get rid of it?

Suddenly, I became aware of the infinite ignorance of man, stewing in hell and believing it to be paradise. This seemed to apply especially to people of Western civilization who "have everything" — money, success, a partner, all varieties of pleasure, a comfortable life without struggle for survival. But how could I describe this seeing to a blind man? What a deception of bliss!

I began to understand why great masters define suffering as sleep. The essential quality of suffering is contained in the fact that the human mind is only marginally aware of its suffering, if at all. This is what is actually fatal about the fall of man. In the moment of falling, blindness becomes blind to blindness, and being unconscious of unconsciousness becomes the human condition. The almost perfect illusion of relative happiness and presumed love is actually confounded by comfort, well-being, and transient pleasures.

In the months after my first encounter with Gangaji, I met with a therapist several times in order to explore, through the help of transpersonal states, the true facts of my accident. To both our surprise, the accident itself had not left any tension or strain on me. As often as I returned to the actual event, the mind remained quiet and there was no reaction. The fact that only ten days after my awakening from the coma I was able to relax in the car and even drive myself showed that the accident had left no trace of trauma in the mind.

Finally, my companion urged me to try to understand what had happened by once again going back through the accident, step by step, in slow motion and total awareness, from the moment I'd gotten into the car. When I remembered the sensation that arose while I was driving my Mercedes through the nighttime streets of Hamburg, the stereo turned all the way up, it happened. The mind reacted with extreme irritation and an intensely biting thought shot up from the depths: "I will decide for myself when I am going to die." It was shocking. For a moment we kept an embarrassed silence. Then my companion offered a comment that at that moment was meant humorously, but only to a degree, "Well, you really put a spoke through the Old Man's wheel." The sarcasm naturally played down the incredible megalomania of that thought.

I felt a rare mixture of disgust and lightness of heart. In this moment, I knew that the temptation of that old misled desire for power, which I had tried to attain by the means of black magic, had definitely been cut. The dissolution of the pact had been the first step, and the realization after the accident had shown the absurdity of that desire.

In the time that followed this experience, the deepest recognitions about Dervish's personal story of suffering were set free. The concept of guilt was revealed to be the original trauma of the mind. This realization had never before been accessible to me, and I was surprised when shown that the terror, this ungraspable, sneaking fear that had been my constant companion, was built upon a foundation of guilt.

I reported to Gangaji in a letter:

"An idea called "Dervish" had a desire for power in order to raise himself above the divine. Then, the feeling of shame that arose in the face of the Almighty caused the desire for humbleness to also arise."

Once this foundation of guilt had been exposed, the movie of Dervish's life showed itself in a new light. It became clear that any motivation in his life was a subconscious attempt to escape guilt. Past occurrences suddenly appeared in consciousness connected by this invisible thread of guilt. Even as a young boy, he often had feelings of deep guilt. The actual events to which the guilt was attached were of no importance. Even his search for truth and entrance upon a spiritual path proved later to be a desperate attempt to rid himself of the heavy burden of guilt. The idea of self-purification had determined Dervish's work with his first teacher, a North African Sufi. In an old diary, I found an entry from that time:

> ". . . Therefore it is important for me to go on working mercilessly on my self-purification. By "self-purification," I mean:
>   1. The purification of my heart through the help of Sufi methods and prayers.
>   2. The work on all my weaknesses, negative qualities, areas of emotional restlessness, and strong desires on the material plane.
>   3. The physical purification of the body through fasting and other yogic methods.

Almost in the same breath, he had denied the guilt: "Do I feel guilt about myself?" he questioned. "No, an excessive guilt complex has actually never been my problem."

Now, in this current experience of giving up the denial of guilt, I had the sensation of falling directly into the layers of original guilt.

About a year after the accident and a short time before I was going to meet Gangaji again, I encountered guilt one last time on a journey of inner exploration. This time it was not bound to concrete inner images but appeared as feelings of deep uncertainty and guilt about "original sin," which I recognized as the belief in separation from the divine Self. The original reason for the concept of guilt seemed to have been exposed, and it burnt away in consciousness without identification. Out of that, for the first time, the blossom of no guilt opened into innocence and I felt that no one had ever been guilty.

The Birth of the Lion

In August 1991, I traveled again to Lunz-am-See in Austria to meet with Gangaji who was again holding Satsang there. During the day, I took part in a therapeutic training. In the evenings, I sat with Gangaji in Satsang. Since meeting Gangaji the year before, I had been in continuous correspondence with her. The fact that I had been led to her right after the accident was a powerful confirmation and created an immense excitement in me. My chance seemed to have come, perhaps for the first time in millions of years! I knew that I had to make use of it. It was now or never. I felt as if a great vortex of energy pulled me towards Gangaji. My home, my heart, seemed to be within arm's reach. Here, for the first time as a student, I became aware of the unconditional totality required in a true relationship to the teacher. My life, or more precisely, what remained of it, had been essentially reduced to this relationship. I understood that Gangaji *is* that which I had searched for.

A force of great fear arose. Naked fear. The fear of an inconceivable loss that was like an opening abyss. Something in me felt strongly threatened.

In Satsang, Gangaji had spoken of the necessity to totally give oneself up to *Shakti*.* "She will take care of everything," Gangaji said. At the end of the Satsang I had the arrogance to tell her I hoped Shakti would take care of my wishes too. The next morning Gangaji expressed her deep concern about this arrogance.

Unfathomable fears of loss had been opened inside me, and along with this came an awareness of deeply conditioned concepts of enlightenment. These concepts sketched enlightenment as an ascetic, unworldly state, prohibiting any form of sensual pleasure. Past incarnations as a monk pushed their way to the surface. Although these fears and images no longer held the power of blind identification, a seemingly solid residue of identification remained, and the sense of a threat was undeniable.

Physically, I was just as far from recovery as before. The exterior wounds had healed fast, it was true, and I had not sustained any internal injuries, but the whole energetic system of the body had collapsed. At times, I had almost no physical energy at my disposal. There were lasting states of weakness and exhaustion. The cerebral command center of the nervous system no longer seemed to function. The smallest physical or mental effort immediately overcharged the system so that I was continuously forced to rest and do nothing. It was frustrating, and yet, in the background of my awareness was a knowing that this was essential in order to dedicate my whole attention to the one true longing, the longing for final freedom.

Satsang with Gangaji made very clear the state in which I found myself. Consciousness had liberated itself from attachment to the physical plane, and there was almost no identification with the emotions. I had attained a state of constant dissociation in which I observed all occurring phenomena without identifying them as "me." I observed the body move and act. I was a witness to emotional states and thoughts. Most of my attention was still directed towards them, yet the splitting of the mind into conscious and unconscious appeared to be dissolved, and I was aware of each thought appearing and then disappearing. All these appearances were of great clarity, no longer dim, distorted, or numb as before. The self-narcotization of the mind no longer seemed to function, so there was no hiding place in my consciousness for either feelings or thoughts.

At times this nakedness was extremely uncomfortable. I still felt very caught in the fixation of being the observer, particularly the seeming reality of the I-thought, and this was painful. On a level that I could not understand, identification with the I-thought was not dissolved by states of dissociation.

After about two weeks with Gangaji, something unforeseen suddenly happened. The area that until then I had taken for the "place of perception" suddenly descended from the head to the chest. All of a sudden, I seemed to perceive the world from the heart center. This way of perception seemed more direct. I felt deep love for everything and everyone, and at times everything seemed to melt into everything else.

At the same time, a fire started to burn in my chest. A fire of longing had been kindled and it grew into a raging wildfire. It was like an immense vacuum, taking thoughts, feelings, and even the outside world and swallowing them. Everything began to melt into this longing. As a thought, the question, "What do I want?" no longer held any importance. I was only this immense longing. It was overwhelming. But this longing was not like any longing I had previously known. It was a longing that did not long for anything, a pure longing in which pain and bliss were no longer separate.

For three days and three nights the fire burned. I explained to the participants of the training that I could not take part in the group anymore, as any therapeutic exercise or even conversation with other members of the group would take me away from the awareness of this fire.

One tepid summer evening in August 1991, Gangaji held Satsang on a mountain meadow under a huge old lime tree. From this vantage point, one had a breathtaking view of the lake of Lunz, which in its silent splendor sunk majestically into the mountains, offering a perfect meditative background for Satsang. In Satsang, I was often too shy to ask questions, and it took great courage to get into dialog with Gangaji in front of the group. Finally, I reported to her the results of my Self-inquiry. I told her that I was able to observe all thoughts, but ultimately this did not help because even in this position I remained a prisoner. I-thoughts still appeared and created suffering. I had to recognize that non-identification was not yet the end of suffering.

Gangaji pointed me inward with the question: *Who is aware of these thoughts?* I was still for a moment, and then suddenly I was seized by an infinite revelation. The reality of the I-thought burst like a soap bubble, and the whole world imploded. In a timeless moment of grace, I recognized the absurd spectacle of ideas that continuously attempt to prove themselves true. From the depths of me, an uncontrollable and unending laughter arose.

That same evening I wrote in a letter to Gangaji:

"All temptations crystallize into a single temptation, the temptation of 'idea' itself."

The essential nature of ideas had been revealed. The whole world is kept together by the I-thought alone, and through uprooting this thought that had never really had a root, the whole world had been uprooted. There was no longer any relationship between "me" and "the world." I was speechless in the face of the unfathomable and grotesque spectacle of life. An ocean of bliss opened within me, and I spent the following days drowning in complete stillness without a single thought.

Some days later, I received the inner guidance that I should travel to India and meet with Gangaji's teacher, Poonjaji, in order to deepen my realization.

On September 6th, 1991, I arrived in New Delhi and on the following day traveled to Lucknow where Poonjaji resided. This was my first journey to India. Before this time, I had never felt attracted to going there.

After arriving in Lucknow, I found accommodations at a shabby former luxury hotel built in English colonial style. Half of the guests were visitors from Western countries who had come to see Poonjaji. The next morning, I went to Poonjaji's house by rickshaw. Chaos reigned in the streets. Cows, sheep, and other objects I couldn't identify lay quietly in the middle of the road. Pedestrians, rickshaws, and car drivers seemed to share the main street with equal rights. Surprisingly, this chaotic arrangement functioned quite well.

I stepped into the stillness of Shri Poonjaji's living room where he was holding Satsang. About fifty people were present and filled the room up to the last corner. Until recently, Shri Poonjaji had been an unknown Indian master who for many years held Satsang with ten or less students. But then he had been discovered by Osho-disciples who, after Osho's death, had been keeping an eye out for a new teacher.

While Osho's teachings for many of them had provoked the misunderstanding that enlightenment was practically unobtainable, here, suddenly, was a teacher who informed the seekers that in reality they were already enlightened and that it was possible to give up the search *now*. This message, of course, fit in with many Osho-disciples who considered enlightenment to be a game that was about having as much fun as possible. Among the first visitors, however, were also some Osho-Sannyasins who had left behind the enlightenment "game," who had *got it*, and who were totally changed by their experience with Shri Poonjaji. These people would reappear at the Osho ashram in Pune, only to turn their backs on the ashram shortly thereafter.

These occurrences started many rumors in Pune. The management of the ashram was deeply concerned about the fact that there now seemed to be some enlightened ones who had actually *gotten it*. Obviously threatened by the scope of this kind of influence, they tried to keep Osho-disciples from visiting Shri Poonjaji, even going so far as to officially announce that it was undesirable to go and see Shri Poonjaji. It didn't help. In the worldwide, extremely well-functioning network of Osho-Sannyasins, the news of a master that "made enlightenment available" spread like wildfire. To this day, many of those still on the spiritual search were once students of Osho.

After I had greeted Shri Poonjaji and given him a long letter I had written, I quietly sat down on a cushion in the back row of the room. The meeting with Shri Poonjaji, whom I recognized at once as my own *Self*, was not particularly spectacular. In fact, it did not really seem to happen *in form* because I no longer experienced myself as present in a particular form. Since the moment of my realization in Satsang with Gangaji, I witnessed an inner process in which everything that had name and form was rejected as "not reality." Everything that appeared as an object in consciousness, at this point primarily the "outside world," was empty, and thus without any importance. Naturally, then, "other people" also counted as "objects," for they were revealed to be imaginary beings without any reality except that created by the mind. The world appeared as a phantom theatre. Bodies walked around like empty shells, and behind the scenes there was—Nothing.

"I" no longer experienced "relationship" with anything or anybody. Everything was equally valid, or even closer yet, invalid. Life or death no longer meant anything. At this point, the impulse to take care of the body had become very weak. The instinct for self-preservation was withdrawing. It was as if all my energy was pulling back into itself, withdrawing from this theatre of images I had previously taken as reality. Without having any desire to connect with Poonjaji as a person, the source of the deepest recognition began bubbling inside me as not separate from the wisdom speaking through his mouth.

In my letter to Poonjaji the evening before, I had described the course of events leading to the experience of awakening. During the next Satsang, Poonjaji read my letter out loud:

"Dervish could give birth to any thought he liked, for it was he, himself, who decided what was "true" or "not true." It is the mind that makes the mind come true, the snake that bites into its own tail. I also recognize that within the dream, every perception is connected with a thought. No matter whether it is about 'inner' or 'outer' perception, the bubble of perception can be traced back to an initial thought. This bubble of perception is what Dervish once called 'reality,' an image of himself that was reflected everywhere. Dervish had always taken this process for granted, as he had never questioned who it was that created this reality. In this light, the phrase from the Bible, 'In the beginning was the word,' could be understood. To be precise, it was not the 'word' but the 'thought,' the I-thought. The word is just the spoken thought."

Poonjaji's comment was: "This required confirmation." Confirmation was essential, indeed, the confirmation of my own heart, which was reflected in the form of Shri Poonjaji. The mind, or what remained of it as reality, could hardly believe *it*. In the following two days, I was catapulted into the deepest confusion and doubt. Poonjaji's presence relentlessly brought up the "dregs" of the mind from shadow into daylight.

On the third day I wrote to Gangaji:

"The first days here were really hard. The confusion was so complete that I really no longer knew what was going on. The full spectrum of the character fixation showed in all its splendor. Demons appeared in all the facets of the rainbow. Last night, out of nowhere, recognition occurred, and the knot that seemed inextricable was suddenly untied. The whole complicated story revealed itself as a mere repetition of the one temptation, the temptation of seeking. In this case, seeking for enlightenment. The demon of doubt tried to make me forget that I had already found."

When I stated that nothing had any validity or worth anymore, this was not quite correct. At first I had experienced the process of retreating from the world as the withdrawing of life energy from outside phenomena, but at some point after that, there was also a retreat from the appearance of inner phenomena such as thoughts, feelings, and sensations. At the core of the remaining inner processes was a deepening of realization. Everything seemed to retreat to that core and to serve it.

At the end of the first week in India, I had a dream: Face to face with a friend, I stood at the edge of an abyss and together we jumped into the depths. While I was falling, I recognized there was no bottom. Waves of fear rushed through me as I said repeatedly like a mantra, "*I am, I am, I am . . .*" as if I had to assure myself that I could fall into nothingness, into the bottomless, and yet *be*.

Poonjaji asked me into his bedroom and told me that from now on I belonged to his family. In a strange way, I was not receptive to "exterior communication." I felt neither joy nor passion for anything, not even for Poonjaji as a person. Feelings seemed to be stunted. Without feeling a need to be close to Poonjaji as a person, I was closer to him than close. This was not an emotional closeness, however, but an absorption into the *one* consciousness.

In the time that followed the body became very sick. It contracted bronchitis and a high fever. The body burned and became increasingly weaker. I could no longer find an "I" involved in this process in any way. It happened without the doing of an "I."

The last day before my departure, I handed another letter to Poonjaji, which he opened during Satsang. He pulled an empty sheet of paper out of the envelope. The laughter among the people present was great and Poonjaji took sheer pleasure in it. "I can understand this language very well," he commented, and he repeated this several times. With a sense of farewell in the heart, I left Lucknow, knowing very well that this was no farewell from my teacher.

Burning in Nothingness

In October 1991, I returned to Germany. Even though it looked exactly as before, everything had changed. The uprooting of the I-thought had carried everything else along with it. Memory had been torn from its anchorage. The stream of time no longer existed as reality. The whole dimension of time was realized to have been only a construct of the I-thought. All objects of perception existed only in the moment of perceiving them. In the next moment, nothing real remained of them. Things from the past, such as old friends and acquaintances, were like phantoms. Nevertheless, I met with them totally, naturally, and spontaneously out of the moment, out of the all pervading *I am*. I saw that other people lived almost completely out of the past, and in the moment of our meeting, they did not truly meet me but rather their own projections of who they thought I was.

It was like being a ghost. There was no longer anyone that dwelled in my body, no supposed I, no supposed soul, and naturally, there never had been. I was neither inside nor outside the body and experienced the powerful stillness and self-evidence of the all-embracing *I am*.

I wrote to Gangaji:

"Within this dream that called himself Dervish, there happened, it seems, the following story: When this idea of Dervish was born, he took off in a plane. He seemed to be the pilot. Suddenly, who knows why, he realized that he was not the pilot. Even worse, this 'he' had only been an idea, an idea that confirmed its own version of truth. After all, the whole flight was revealed to be a dream. 'I' returned to the place from where I had never started out.
Now, within the dream, the flight goes on and the plane flies by itself. The new 'owner' is simultaneously the flyer, the flown, and the flight. The direction of the plane may change, but nobody knows where to."

The communication I witnessed between people turned out to be more like a grotesque comedy, reminding me of Monty Python movies. Everyone pretended to know who they were, referred to themselves totally naturally as "I," and then projected this pseudo-knowledge outside themselves. The reversal, meaning "negatives" of arbitrary self-concepts, also then appeared on the "outside" as the "other" with whom communication takes place. This process is called "relationship" and "communication." To make a long story short, the "relationship" between two people is, in reality, a relationship between two sets of self-concepts.

I saw that everyone lives in a preconception of himself or herself, like in a personal dream, a soap bubble, the limits of which are defined by the amount of one's ignorance of one's true nature, by the degree of the loss of Reality. Most encounters take place only within this soap bubble. No one really knows who is actually communicating with whom. My interest in seriously taking part in this play was completely exhausted, even though it sometimes appeared entertaining, comical, and because of that, lovable.

I recognized that human characters are a hodgepodge of mostly subconscious images, clung to by memory, and which overlay the suchness of the moment. Sometimes this cover of clouds made of images and preconceptions seemed to spontaneously tear open, and I saw how people, without any conscious realization of Self, dwelled totally naturally in suchness. This happened, for instance, in moments and situations that were truly comical. In such a moment of *No-Mind,** true communication happens in the sense of communion, the sharing of heart to heart, Self to Self. Poonjaji had always stressed the importance of laughing. In the moment of laughter, the mind has no chance of prevailing.

In my experience, "I" had no fixed identity as a "somebody." I could no longer describe how I was, which qualities I had, how I should behave, or how I shouldn't. Everything that had once formed my fixed identity had been surrendered to the unknown and was therefore unpredictable. Never known facets of my inner life appeared in quick succession. Emotional states, images, and thoughts followed each other, just to burn away in consciousness without leaving a trace behind. Negative states were as much a part of my experience as positive states, but different from earlier times, they never lasted for long. The core dualism of the mind, with its split into conscious and subconscious, no longer functioned so that every negative thought and every unpleasant feeling appeared in consciousness naked and undistorted. Their hiding place had been taken away.

Moments of suffering caused by subtle re-identification with thoughts were immediately obvious and painful. These moments became extremely subtle, like filigree. They were moments of incomplete vigilance in which occurred an energetic connection, a relationship between consciousness and a thought or a feeling. In an instant, something that I can only describe as a kind of energetic "hooking in" was triggered by an invisible power. The result was immediate duality. What was this invisible power?

Through the realization of true Self, the mind, the supposed "I," dissolves into nothing. In other words, it reveals its nature as a phantom, a ghost. A phantom is empty by nature and without any substance. Because complete realization does not in truth exist, and realization can only approach completeness, the mind continues to exist on more and more subtle levels. I would call it the mind's "after-pains," which follow realization just as every birth is followed by after-pains. It was these after-pains of the mind that I sometimes realized as the invisible power at work, creating an immediate experience of separation from true Self and consequent suffering. The immediate awareness of suffering was what brought about the dissolution of all thoughts in the next moment, thus preparing the way for an experience of deepening peace. The moments in which the mind was still at work became

more and more rare, more and more subtle, hardly possible
to be captured in words.

I wrote to Gangaji:

> *"Since the moment in which the world imploded, self-
> exploration takes place in effortless effort, an exploration
> of the most subtle levels of ideas. I recognize that ideas
> penetrate into the most delicate layers of consciousness of
> which I have no conscious awareness. They are traces of
> traces of thoughts."*

Continuous   self-exploration   supported   the
deepening of realization, and at the same time the whole
story of the mind and its million-year-old *karma** was
ablaze. This burning was anything but subtle. It spread
through every level of the organism. In the physical body,
the brain seemed to restructure itself. The body was no
longer the body as it had been known. It seemed to
reassemble. Actually, for a long time, I experienced a kind
of re-materialization of the physical body, like the ethereal
energy was being recompressed. Directly after awakening
from the coma, and in the time afterwards, the subjective
body no longer had any weight.

The first years after the accident were dominated by
an immense feeling of physical "sickness." I can't describe
it otherwise. I experienced a pervasive feeling of sickness,
without any specific reason, and not even restricted to any
particular area or system of the body. Experiences of old
karma burning away alternated with states of deep, still joy
and bliss. Eventually, with the return of the physical
energy, a process that would subsequently take about six
years, a sensation of grounded solidity and power
occurred, which was at the same time very calming.

On the 11th of November, 1991, I wrote to Gangaji:

"Every wave that manifests returns to this unimaginable joy of pure being – Being, consciousness, love, truth, emptiness . . . it is all the same overwhelming joy of the presence of the eternal Being. It is as if the deepest aspects of the character fixation are manifesting and burning away. I experience states of immense, bottomless, naked fear, not knowing about what, and extreme feelings of vulnerability and shame. All of that appears on its own, without being triggered by anything in particular, and then dissolves once again. What has become entangled disentangles on its own, as soon as the mind returns to stillness."

The dregs of the subconscious that had settled there for millions of years were stirred and carried up into the light of consciousness. This must have happened to the Buddha who, while sitting under the bodhi tree after his enlightenment, met all the demons of his personal story. But Gangaji had hammered it into my head, and I had listened very carefully, "Whatever appears, don't touch it!" Thus, all the demons, as extensive and seemingly real as they appeared, were revealed to be empty, inflated ghosts that deflated on their own. These inner demons were like phantoms in the most magnificent robes, carried by nothingness. And from nothing – comes nothing.

Back in the Marketplace

I found myself in a state of infinite astonishment, in the stillness of No-Mind. No dangers existed, no temptations, no unfulfilled desires, nor any suffering.

I asked in a letter to Gangaji:

"Can any unfulfilled desire exist without a thought first
breaking through stillness? If vigilance allows the initial
thought to fall back into emptiness, if it does not allow a
single thought to cut thru the stillness, then it seems
neither important to reject an unfulfilled desire nor even
to recognize it, because it simply does not exist.
No letting go of the ego.
No rejection of attachments.
No cutting away of unfulfilled wishes.
Just pure realization.
A thought, so tiny,
hardly worth mentioning,
and yet . . .
the moment it arises,
a powerful demon
claims the truth for himself.
It was what it had never been:
An idea that gave truth to other ideas.
An absurd, self-fulfilling play.
A never-ending cycle of suffering:
Samsara."

Now, as before, it was very important for me to
write to Gangaji. I called these letters, "Letters from Self to
Self." In this way, inexplicably, the Self had discovered a
way to teach itself, to deepen the realization of itself.

Gangaji had said, "Those who have had experiences
of enlightenment are like the hair of a buffalo. Those who
have attained complete realization are like the horns of a
buffalo." This statement had made an indelible impression
on me. Also the statement: "As long as this body of desires
appears, temptation also appears." I began to explore the
apparent contradiction of immediate, timeless awakening
and the deepening of realization as a process in time—a
koan*.

"It seems to me that the structures of the mind reach much deeper, become much subtler, than most seekers assume. Isn't the moment of awakening frequently just a glimpse? It's true that the cycle of suffering can be interrupted by a very deep glimpse, yet the mind has the tendency of landing once again by being satisfied with the relative peace it has attained. The 'I have got it!' becomes a trap. Yes, there is absolute freedom when the Self has been realized. In truth, there is. And yet, in the dream of this 'reality,' 'relative freedom' can deepen. This deepening is not necessarily comfortable, as it requires facing the subtlest shadow concepts of the mind, which do not necessarily correspond to one's 'image of enlightenment.'

The widespread misunderstanding about enlightenment seems to be that enlightenment is considered to be an end, an absolute finish. Yes, it is an end, yet it is also just a beginning. The mind cannot solve this contradiction. It comes sneaking in and uses 'Everything is all the same' as a pretext for landing again. The temptation continues . . ."

Thus I continued to witness a "personal" process of deepening. During this process, neurotic material still appeared, but I was neither identified with it nor separate from it. The simplicity and naturalness of the course of events, and the recognition of perfection in imperfection, were overwhelming.

"Life is a self-fulfilling process. Shakti appears as a thousand-headed hydra; the form of 'human being' is just one of her heads. The idea of an individual 'I' as a doer, a creator, a controller of life, appears absurdly ridiculous. The unknown happens anyway! An old saying reveals

this in a very simple way: Man proposes, God disposes."

In the spring of 1993, I suddenly received an inner command to give up everything within six weeks and go to the United States for an indefinite period of time. There, I experienced a time of great stillness and retreat. I became witness to a contest between opposing forces. My interest in the world was sometimes so weak that even the instinct for self-preservation withdrew. There was no energy to keep up the body. Out of these states of stillness, which coincided with total, physical weakness, again and again a sudden impulse burst forth. In a letter to Gangaji I described this impulse as the "celebration."

> *"Nothing is really of any importance.*
> *After an intense destruction of the world, which happened without my doing, the world now returns as a celebration of Self. There is no longer any accentuation of emptiness beyond form, as* Being *has realized itself as existing within and beyond form. I realize that emptiness itself can be imitated by the mind as 'intentional emptiness.'*
> *Actually, the mind can perfectly copy everything up to the subtlest manifestations of the good, which are as well the natural appearances of the divine* Self. *It seems as if the identification with evil, with the bad, is the root of the mind that leads back to the fall of man, to the original sin. During this illusory process of searching within time, a gradual transformation occurs until the identification with the good is dropped. The good seems to hit much closer to freedom, but still contains within itself the polarity of the bad. Lucifer serves the last temptation on a golden tray, the temptation of the appearance of the good*

as a disguise of God himself. Only very few seem to be ready to tear down this last mask of the good and surrender to the absolute, which contains the bad as well as the good. What has been considered "bad" is connected to the concept of guilt. For me, the painful experience of guilt was like a guard to the gates of absolute freedom."

"Intentional emptiness," the tendency of being attached to non-attachment, dissolved in this realization.

Meanwhile, Gangaji refused to call me by the name Dervish. I received letters from her addressed to Parkin, without any first name. I understood and sent a letter to Shri Poonjaji in India, asking him to give me a new name. Months later, I received a card from India with the salutation, "Dear OM," the name of the nameless one.

In March 1994, I traveled to the mountains of Colorado to meet with Gangaji in a retreat. The impulse to return to Europe for the turn of the year had already appeared. In some moments it seemed to me like the return into the jaws of the lion, and a deep fear kept arising again and again. A few weeks before the retreat, I had communicated to Gangaji that I had started working on the concept of a book. The working title was *The Myth of Enlightenment.* I had asked for a dharma conversation with her, which I intended to publish, and proposed the retreat as a possible date. I finished the letter by asking her for a message. No answer. Nothing.

Crestone was a tiny village at the end of an immensely expanded plateau. Here, huge herds of buffalo became alive in my mind's imagination. Immense vastness was all around. Behind the village, the mountains of more than three thousand meters reached to the sky. I breathed in the beauty and grandeur of this place. It was still.

One morning at the retreat, sitting in Satsang with Gangaji, I became aware of a subconscious tension slowly arising inside me. It was the mind, but it was not yet revealing itself. In this Satsang, Gangaji told her story of meeting Papaji (Poonjaji). He had waited for her to come and had, so to speak, appointed her his successor in the West. As his new student, he had given her presents, he had loved her, and he had courted her. She was the queen. On her next visit, she could hardly wait to see him again. She demonstrated her attitude by opening her arms and puffing herself up as if to say, "Papaji, here I am again—the one you have waited for!" But Papaji had been totally uninterested and had sent her away, remarking laconically that he was busy with more important things at the moment. For days he had no time for her. What a shock!

While she was telling this, it seemed to me that this story was a perfect tactic by my teacher in order to pull up into consciousness the remainders of my ignorance.

Dearest Gangaji,

*Crestone, 9*th *of March, 1994*
        "This morning during Satsang, I was hit once again by the ruthlessness of the teaching. At that moment a gigantic inner laughter shot up and devoured everything. What a cosmic joke! Here is the story:
        An unfulfilled desire (there it is again!), a desire for confirmation, worked as a cover for subtle layers of doubt. I did not identify with these doubts, yet neither did I realize they were there. These were thoughts that had not yet come to the surface, but were held back subconsciously — "I can't do that . . . I am not yet ripe for it . . . etc. "They have to do with my knowing that I have to return to Europe to be in Satsang, to give Satsang, to live Satsang. This story about a person who doesn't actually exist, how subtle it becomes! How many confirmations have I received already? From Poonjaji, from Gangaji, from my inner teacher, continuously. The truth is, confirmation does not exist! What I am needs no confirmation!

Well, it seems that I will have to return to Europe in order to do what has to be done. To hold Satsang if Satsang is to be held. To not hold Satsang if no Satsang is to be held. To write this book if it has to be written. And so on.

There is the realization of what it means to be totally thrown back on oneSelf. Aloneness; all-one-ness. It is in this total innocence that I cry out, "I AM nobody else but the Lord Himself!" This, Gangaji, is the grandeur and the ordinariness of what I am.

I speak through your mouth, because it is mine. This is the no-place where I meet you not as a student, not as a teacher, not even as a brother. As yourSelf.

Thank you for this teaching. Words cannot reach it.

In Love, Being, and with a gigantic inner smile,"

OM

DIALOGUES OF SELF-INQUIRY

Satsang

Welcome to Satsang. Please feel invited to ask a question any time. If you ask a question, I will answer it for you. *Who* asks the question and *who* answers it?

You believe I am a person living in this body and answering your question. If you identify with your body as "I," you believe that I am a body too. This is the origin of separation. Separation brings about loss, which makes all humans feel cut off from their source, and this illusion has to be dissolved. When you ask a question, the answer you receive is not given by a person, for this body here is only one of my persons. Person, or persona, means "mask." What do you know about yourself? What do you know about me? As I am no individual, the answer is impersonal. I am *yourSelf.*

If you want to be still, please feel invited to be still. I am not saying that you necessarily keep your mouth shut, but that you keep quiet within your thoughts. This is the only thing to do anyway, if it's possible to say there is something to do at all. If anyone has a serious interest in bringing suffering to an end, it is necessary only to be still. Suffering is exclusively a question of thoughts. It is possible for thoughts to calm down without anyone having to do anything about it, without anyone having to sit down and meditate, although there is nothing wrong with meditating. I'm saying that it is possible, at this moment, to relax one's mind* without any effort so that the thoughts simply settle down. If thoughts settle down, if everything settles down, what remains? Usually, the mind is so intensely and continuously occupied with phenomena that there is no possibility of calming down.

It was my good luck that for one moment this trance of phenomena, of images and motion, settled down. At that moment, everything that remained was my *Self*.

In a certain way, I have nothing to tell you. I am not saying, however, that I have nothing to communicate. I just don't have a teaching to spread. No teaching is necessary to learn who you are. The possibility of you recognizing the truth of who you are is only a question of your level of interest, for I have seen repeatedly that for some mysterious reason there is almost no one interested in absolute self-recognition. Most people are interested in teachings, or they are interested in continually new and exciting experiences, extraordinary experiences, physical experiences, emotional experiences, or supernatural experiences. But almost nobody has total interest in realizing the truth about themselves, about their own immortality.

Satsang is the invitation to be at home. You do not come from anywhere, and you do not go anywhere. You are *here*. You are not born and you will not die, you are *here*. In this simplicity, what has to happen, happens, and what does not have to happen, does not happen. There is nothing to do, just total awareness, total vigilance in the face of temptation. Gangaji once compared it to a cat sitting in front of a mouse-hole. Whenever a mouse comes out of the hole, she is present. The mice are thoughts. As soon as the cat falls asleep, as eventually will happen, and gets lost in nonessentials, the thoughts come sneaking out and peace is gone.

Satsang begins where concept and ideologies end. Questions that arise from concepts can only ask "what?" or "why?" or "how?" Satsang asks the question "who?."

The nature of Satsang is not controversial, but it creates controversy because it questions all the fixed ideas of the mind. You can question everything, but often the problem in truly hearing the answer is that the mind swings back and forth between belief and doubt. First you believe something, then you doubt it. According to your habit, either gullibility or doubt will prevail. Satsang is the *crack*, the crack between doubt and belief. In this crack, it is neither necessary to doubt nor to believe.

When you are in this crack, you are open for the first time. In this openness, you are ready for Satsang. When the mind first comes to Satsang, it is not open. It is loaded with opinions, speculations, assumptions, beliefs, doubts, interpretations, and knowledge. But in the middle of the crack, there you are, open for the first time. You need not believe that you know anything, and you need not believe that you don't know anything. You are open. There is nothing to defend, nothing to believe, nothing to doubt.

Satsang is only possible in an attitude of total not knowing. I am not speaking of an attitude of ignorance, but one of truly not knowing. In a certain way, it is a childlike, innocent attitude in which the exploration of reality becomes possible. It is the *don't-know-mind*, a total not knowing that leaves past, present, and future behind, and out of which alone Satsang is possible.

The acquired knowledge, the supposed erudition of the mind is the greatest problem, particularly here in the West. To enter into Satsang is to enter into the total simplicity of *what is* beyond any concepts, as sublime, noble, or credible as those concepts may appear. But who is ready to give up any knowledge and any ignorance from the past? Anything from the past, with no exception, ultimately veils total, open, *not knowing*. This even includes spiritual knowledge.

If you believe you already know everything, how can you learn anything new? Believing to know something is not the attitude in which you are truly ready to receive Satsang. In an attitude of knowing, the mind continually confirms its knowledge to itself and then believes itself to know something.

There are two basic attitudes of the mind that keep you from being in Satsang. The first attitude is "I know something," and the second attitude is "I don't know anything." The mind only knows these polarities. What you call "knowing" is understanding and interpretation, but I do not speak of understanding and interpretation. You touch innocence when you at least understand that you do not understand anything.

The attitude, "I do not know anything," is something different. It is a self-negating attitude that is just the flip side of arrogance. Arrogance is the nature of the *thinking mind,** which believes itself to be separate from *Self*. It is the belief, "I know something," and this knowing just creates arbitrary standards. In its arrogance, the mind comes here to Satsang and believes it knows who "I" am. It believes it knows who "it" is. The arrogant mind believes it knows what it is all about, and whoever is still completely involved with the arrogance of the mind is not ready for Satsang.

When the mind says, "I truly know everything," and this statement can be made in total bliss, then it must be truth. If it contains, however, the effort of having to defend an image that could break down as soon as the effort that artificially keeps this image alive breaks down, you realize that something is not quite reliable. Then you are well advised to no longer believe the mind's, "I know everything," because then it is just a thought. Unfortunately, most of the time, you don't recognize it as just a thought. Thoughts ultimately aren't recognized as thoughts because the reality of Being, Consciousness, and Love, which is beyond thoughts and feelings, is denied, and this is astonishing.

In Satsang, you will have the experience of continuously coming up against contradictions — but only if you are comparing. Comparing is another disease of the mind. If you do not compare, contradictions do not exist. If you are simply with what is now, if you are open to receive what is said in this moment without believing it and without doubting it, then there is the possibility of inner understanding. Inner understanding is possible only when all attempts to understand are given up. It is not an understanding that takes place in the mind. It is an understanding without any words and without any thoughts. It is an understanding in the heart at a place that cannot be localized. It is the moment in which the one who "talks" and the one who "listens" become one. In that moment, inner understanding is possible. As long as you try to understand, as long as you try to weave what I say into the existing intellectual framework of your mind, you are not open to truly hearing.

The *don't-know-mind* is neither in resistance to anything nor does it believe anything. Belief is pure indolence, and unfortunately, many people indulge in this indolence. Complete religions have sprung out of belief. For many people it is easier to believe what the teacher says rather than to self-investigate. Belief and doubt both arise out of mental laziness. Both are very indolent ways to escape the responsibility of personal and direct experience. What is the use of believing anything I say? What is the use of doubting anything I say? If you see a contradiction here, wonderful!

Gangaji has said, "Invite your enemies to Satsang." Invite everything to Satsang, everything that is carried along by indolence, shame, and guilt. If you really invite everything to Satsang, nothing has the power to resist Satsang. Nothing can resist pure consciousness. In Satsang, all of these enemies or demons or concepts of the *thinking mind* are revealed at the core to be false. Invite everything, even chaos, confusion, or disgust. Invite whatever arises without clinging to it and without making a drama out of it. Whatever it is, it is not genuine anyway. It is artificial, an artificial and illusory world that burns away like drifting fog dissolving in sunshine. Consciousness always shines.

When you are in Satsang, when you are in total awareness of everything there is, there is no possibility for the *thinking mind* to survive. Remain in this total vigilance without any effort, and do not touch what arises. Whatever arises, it is not you.

The mind always has an ugly side, and one could say this ugly side is the skeleton in the cupboard of the subconscious. It has been locked away, expelled from consciousness exactly like in the social arena where everything that is not normal is expelled from society. The social arena is only a reflection of the individual mind expelling everything that does not fit its self-created image of what is good and just. In Satsang, this ugly side cannot fail to appear. Naturally, there is a strong temptation to avoid it, because I have often seen that the clinging to negative concepts is much stronger than clinging to positive concepts. Instead, let everything that appears in consciousness burn away in Satsang.

The whole purpose of Darshan is that it can come to an end. It does not need to be maintained. In many religions the original idea, which was also to immediately give up the search, has been changed into maintaining it. My observation is that religious institutions repeatedly fall to the temptation of maintaining themselves. Institutionalized spirituality doesn't make sense to me because its true purpose is not in maintaining itself, but rather in coming to an end. A search that gives itself a sense of maintaining itself is a search that has to confirm itself again and again. How can a religion or an ashram have the pure intention of destroying the search if by that same token the ashram is tempted by the survival instinct to maintain itself? You have to ask yourself this question, for any search is always directed toward some time in the future and not towards *now*, and this is the whole problem.

Satsang is not confined to space and time. Satsang is *here*. When you leave this room, you think Satsang is over, but *here* is not here in this room, and it is not in this moment either. *Here* is *here*.

Suffering

The I-Thought is the Source of Suffering

Ramana Maharshi's central teaching is this: "The identification with the I-thought is the source of suffering." To me, this is one of the clearest statements there is.

* * *

How do the mind and the true I relate to each other? Are they one and the same?

The moment that pure consciousness, which is the true I, became identified with the I-thought, the false I came into existence. I call this false I the *thinking mind*. There is a pact by which consciousness itself has connected with the I-thought, and by the ensuing fall into duality, it has the opportunity to recognize itself. Finally, it is realized that the *thinking mind* and the true I are one and the same.

* * *

What is suffering?

Suffering is an illusion.

Then does humanity suffer simply from an illusion?

Yes. The problem is not suffering itself; the problem is that humanity is not fully aware of it. When every activity of the mind that immediately creates separation and thereby suffering happens in total awareness of yourself, the illusion is exposed and suffering is finished. In other words, when the I-thought appears and you become that thought, it is in that moment suffering is created. But when the I-thought happens in total, conscious awareness, I do not believe you will be interested in following this misidentification.

Suffering does not make itself openly known as suffering. Most people believe that a disease of the body or the psyche creates suffering. When they are able to function again, suffering is supposed to be finished. There are all kinds of techniques and ways to smooth out suffering, to search for pleasure and do something to keep suffering from becoming obvious.

I like Papaji's definition of suffering best: "Suffering is the relationship with the I-thought."

There are continuously arising thoughts attached to the letter *I*, thoughts of which you are not aware but which you become again and again as they arise. These thoughts become what you are, and then feelings and sensations ensue. But are *you* a thought?

Thinking is the only problem. To be even more precise, thinking itself is not the problem; the problem is your attachment to thinking. Your love for thinking is not love for the Self. This relationship with thinking is simply and solely responsible for the suffering in the world. If you are truly interested in giving up suffering, there is nothing that needs to change except to give up this relationship with your thoughts.

What is thinking? Thinking is created by just one thought, and that is the I-thought, a thought that starts with the letter "I" —*I* am such-and-such; *I* am called so-and-so; *I* have this-and-that; *I* want this-and-that; *I* do not want this-and-that. All of these thoughts have a common denominator, and that is this one letter, "I." This letter is fatal. In fact, suffering can be tracked back to the beginning of this initial thought.

If you experience moments in which no I-thought exists, you experience a kind of bliss. In deep sleep, you do not have any experience of suffering. Suffering originates in the moment when the state of consciousness changes, and you enter the so-called waking state. At this moment, the I-thought comes into existence subconsciously.

Who is I? I invite you to look inside now and to watch. What do you perceive when you ask yourself the question, Who am I?

Guilt and Obliviousness

How does guilt come into existence?

Guilt is a consequence of the first I-thought. The first moment that Adam thought himself to be Adam—or in other words, when the first I-thought appeared and identified itself as "Adam" — he suddenly felt naked and separate from God. He experienced shame and guilt.

Many people believe that they have to pass through guilt or through suffering to become really fulfilled and liberated.

This is an old Christian concept still lived in many Christian countries such as Spain. Even today, rituals exist in which the faithful and barefoot drag heavy crosses along for miles and other forms of abjuration. The Christian religion has turned into a religion of suffering.

This mentality is still to be found here in Germany as well.

Naturally, these rituals and "techniques" contain the essence of truth. This essence of truth is what makes the awareness of guilt accessible for the first time. In its normal state, the mind denies guilt. In any case, it is all about making the core of this original guilt accessible, to remove all the peripheral concepts to which guilt always attaches itself so that the original guilt, which appears as guilt towards the Self, can arise and burn away in surrender.
I would say that every egoic structure is based on guilt. Seen in this way, no matter how it appears on the outside, the ego-structure as such is always built on a defect, on a self-destructive basis, for it then functions by continually making attempts to compensate for this guilt or to avoid feeling it.

What does guilt consist of?

Guilt consists of your belief that you are an individual separate from oneness. You are so-and-so, a separate personality. Guilt is the belief that the wave is something different from the ocean. It's as if a wave separates from the ocean and then tries to give itself importance, wants to be considered and acknowledged as a wave. Then, as a wave, it fights against other waves and even against the water, against itself.

The guilt of separation is deeply hidden, and certain layers appear only when you are ready to go deeper. It is the story of the fall of man from which the whole of humanity has emerged. Every birth, the whole existence of the world, is based on the belief in separation. Every birth of a mind is the birth of guilt. There is no process for dissolving guilt. One speaks of paying off guilt, but the idea of paying off guilt is based on the assumption that guilt is real, that separation is real. There is nothing to pay off. It is simply a matter of recognizing that guilt is a concept. What kind of delusion makes you believe you are something different from pure consciousness?

Does guilt arise from my belief that I am separate? Or am I really separate and this is my guilt? If it isn't a process of liberating myself from the guilt of separation or the illusion of separation, what then is it?

It is the moment of recognizing who you *really* are. The guilt consists of the ignorance of man, and this ignorance keeps recreating the guilt. Ignorance literally means ignoring *knowledge*. Ignorance is the *belief* that you either know something or you don't know anything. When you neither know nor not know, and you are simply still in *that which is;* when you relax totally into *Being* itself without any intentions, without any motivations, without any unfulfilled desires, this is the moment of innocence. When you touch innocence, you touch the sweetness of being and you touch *knowledge* itself. Impersonal knowledge. This is the paradox. And that is the moment in which the whole burden, the whole fight, the whole toil of life falls away. It doesn't really even fall away, for it is simply revealed not to exist. Even falling away is too much effort. *It doesn't exist* — full stop.

The whole struggle of every human being is based in some way on counteracting this primal guilt; to deal with it and manipulate it in a way that the core of it doesn't appear in consciousness for it seems intolerable. The struggle spins on and on. Now you can relax, drop out of it, and enter into the stillness of Satsang. No thoughts, no clinging to thoughts, just the simplicity of what in Zen is called *suchness*. And it is really a razor's edge, for there is no possibility for the mind to alleviate guilt. That guilt can be paid off or reduced is a false teaching of the church. Actually, on the contrary, every action to reduce guilt just creates more guilt. In Eastern traditions, this is called karma. When you keep your fingers off the whole play and you are ready to witness the guilt without doing anything about it, it leaves.

When I had the direct experience of penetrating to the moment of original sin, the Fall of Man, at this moment, I perceived pure guilt. There was no longer even the thought of guilt. By my totally allowing this experience, guilt arose like a wave and burnt away. Guilt, as does everything else, burns away in stillness. Only when you are still do all of these things appear. Then the challenge is not to touch any of it, but just to let it all burn away.

It is important not to consider guilt an enemy to be fought against. Guilt is a great ally. When guilt becomes accessible in its purity, it is a great gift because normally everything the mind does, thinks, and feels is an avoidance of guilt. Satsang begins when guilt, too, is recognized as having nothing to do with the reality of oneself. Guilt is needed to keep in place the deep belief, "I am bad." In the mind's subconscious belief, "I am bad," it has to consciously prove to itself that it is good. To be finished with this play, you have to find out, you have to ask yourself, "Do I really want to be free?" Only then is it possible to be liberated from this burden of guilt you carry around.

* * *

Obliviousness is the foundation of guilt, but, of course, obliviousness has even forgotten guilt. Obliviousness is the moment of the fall of man, the moment you have forgotten the truth of yourself, the moment you have forgotten everything, the moment you have fallen asleep. And your sleep has developed structures that you come to Satsang to recognize. The sleep of obliviousness is your dream, and the dream is called "this world" and "me in this world."

Darshan, the meeting in truth with a teacher, serves both to remind you and to cut the trance of obliviousness. Naturally, the world seems so real, so normal, that it seems indestructible. Thus, a radical cut is needed. A kind of shock. Such a shock can only be triggered in the meeting with your *Self* in human form or some other form, and there are only a few, like Ramana, who did not have a teacher in human form.

Obliviousness happens through thoughts. If you do not touch a thought, there is no obliviousness. Obliviousness is the deepest passion of the human mind. Not only is it the cause of all suffering, but it is the fuel that keeps suffering alive.

Obliviousness is like radioactivity. You do not smell it, you do not see it, and you do not feel it. It becomes perceptible only much later, after it has already done its work of destruction. The power of the mind, also known as the devil, has the same quality as radioactivity. It is an active process cloaked as passivity. Everything seems as if it is just happening. In reality, you are *creating* it, but it has been cloaked so skillfully that it does not appear as if you are doing anything. Therefore, for a certain period of time, it is possible that a spiritual practice is needed to help uncloak the workings of the mind. In any case, what is needed is a teacher, who is, of course, no one else but yourself, no matter what form the teacher appears in.

The driving force behind obliviousness could be called indolence, but then the question remains as to what is the driving force behind indolence. This question can only be answered in a relative way. As absurd as it may sound, in the end the driving force is the desire to suffer, or in other words, the half-hearted desire to be free.

The Desire for Suffering

Freedom is about consciously recognizing the unconscious desire to be limited, the desire to be in prison. This is not a simple desire. This desire has hardened so much it has become an addiction.

Is this desire for imprisonment a punishment?

Naturally, the concept of punishment is also an aspect of the desire to suffer. Although it is admittedly contradictory and incomprehensible, the moment that suffering is obviously here, the desire for suffering must also be present. You voluntarily connect with everything you want to connect with in the universe, be it inside or outside. Or do you really think it is God who wants you to suffer? If you believe this, then you hold God responsible.

But who is "God?" God is just *your* idea of God. You can always only hold your own idea of God responsible and pretend not to be responsible for it yourself.

Surely, nobody wants to suffer. This idea seems really absurd to me.

The desire to suffer does not reveal itself as a desire to suffer. It appears as a desire to be happy. You just don't recognize the disguise, that's all. It can appear, for instance, as a desire to immigrate to another country or an unfulfilled desire for a child or an assumed soul mate. Every unfulfilled desire directed toward something impermanent can never be a *true* desire. If your desire is directed toward something impermanent, once you obtain that object, you will lose it—if not in the next moment, then in some moment in the future. This is necessarily so. How, then, can you take for granted that your desire for happiness will be fulfilled when the necessary result is loss?

Is it not true that behind all these false desires is ultimately only one desire, the desire for identity? Isn't the main desire the desire to be somebody? Whether there is pain or suffering or fear, is not the underlying cause always the desire to be somebody?

Yes, this is true. The desire to be somebody is always a cloaked desire to suffer. Find out if this is your true desire, your final desire. It requires great effort to be somebody. How easy everything is when you no longer have this need. How simple everything becomes when you meet with *Being* itself without having to be "somebody."

Does it mean that I have to give up my individuality?

No, it means giving up being somebody, which means giving up being special. Only by suffering can a person make him or herself into something special. This sense of specialness naturally dissolves in Satsang in the recognition that there is no one who could feel special. What if there is no one special anymore? What if you lose your identity? The identity you have given yourself is an illusory identity anyway. It is a soap bubble. In other words, it is simply and solely a lie.

* * *

Suffering overwhelms me. I am simply overcome by my feelings. I don't seem to have the choice to suffer or not to suffer.

If you don't feel you have a choice, there is still not a complete recognition that you are the doer responsible for your feelings. The responsibility of the doer is denied. You are still using a trick of projecting the doer onto something else without being fully aware of the process. When you completely recognize you are the doer, then you are free either to do or to refrain from doing. Then the experience is no longer, "It happens to me! Depression overwhelms me! Feelings of guilt overcome me!" Suddenly it is recognized, "I myself produce feelings of guilt! Consciously, voluntarily, I actively produce suffering."

Most likely I would understand and see this more easily if I were capable of consciously stopping it.

Yes, exactly, you are not able to consciously stop it as long as you do not completely recognize you are the one responsible for what is being done. The recognition of the responsibility of the doer is prevented, as I already stated, by various tricky mechanisms, deceptions within the structures of the *thinking mind.**

The basic mechanism by which this recognition is prevented is projection. Not projection from the inside onto the outside, as psychology understands it, but projection within the inside. This means, for instance, that without even noticing you project the responsibility of the doer onto a thought, suddenly, the thought is the doer. The personified thought appears as the doer and acts against you. Naturally, once light is shed on you yourself as the doer, all of that no longer makes sense. It is absurd. Actually, it is more than a bad joke, for you would not voluntarily and continually be the creator of suffering.

Unless you have the idea of getting something out of creating suffering. In the course of my life, this has been confirmed and supported from all sides.

This is true. The most essential reason for suffering is that you believe you will win something by it. This belief is the promise of suffering. It is the reason why people *choose* suffering even though they *do not have to suffer.*

Can this be seen as related to the world's political situation, when there is a threat of war, for instance, or when somebody running amuck on the highway shoots at cars and people? Is there ultimately in these people the desire for suffering? And is it the same with unforeseen events like accidents?

Yes, of course, the desire for suffering relates to everything. If something like that happens, there must have been the desire that something like that would happen. Naturally, all kinds of desires exist. In their essence, desires are nothing but the divine play, the multiple, various forms of Self-expression. This world is a play of desires. The true nature of desire is not personal. However, as long as it appears like that, as long as there is someone identified as a person, the desire appears to be personal. Whenever someone is hurt or attacked, whenever someone becomes a victim of violence, there must have been a subconscious desire for violence.

Does this apply also to a child who becomes a victim of violence?

Yes. This applies also to children. Maybe it would be easier for you to imagine it this way: There is a seed-like predisposition for these desires, which in the course of personal development are "hatched" or "developed" in the truest sense of the word. The information has been stored and it will later express itself, which means, it will develop.

Does it mean that ultimately nothing happens accidentally?

That is correct.

So, are there collective desires?

Yes. There is a collective level of the *thinking mind*, and desires can also appear in the social arena, within a state, within a group, within a sub-society, or possibly even on a global scale. The desire to suffer is a collective desire that encompasses all civilizations and societies, for it is the ancient opponent of the desire to be free. But as long as the desire to suffer is suppressed — and this is normally the case — as long as the desire appears in such a cloaked way that there is no conscious approach to suffering, you fall a victim to the false hopes that accompany these desires.

The Denial of Suffering

You say we cling to suffering like to a dead fish. Why do we do so?

    You probably have your reasons for it. Suffering is not what you thought it was before now. Isn't it true that you become aware of suffering only when you feel bad? For years, you have been feeling good. You have had wonderful friends. You have been making good progress in your job. You have been getting along very well with your family. You have been earning a lot of money. Through positive thinking, you have found an apartment without any problem. Everything has been running like clockwork. Do you understand? You have had no real reason to suffer.

    One day, maybe years later, you notice a certain void. You think, "Wait a minute, my affirmations don't work any more. Should I double them, perhaps?" And some day you reach the point of intuiting that there is something fishy going on. For most people, however, it doesn't just take years but hundreds of years for the simple recognition that they are suffering. They haven't realized this before because suffering is quite a baffling mechanism directed by someone whose name I don't even want to mention here: the ruler of the world who sells hell for paradise. Suffering is a very baffling mechanism that can only function because suffering also appears in the disguise of well-being. If suffering stood in front of you nakedly, suffering would have no possibility of continuing. Suffering continues only by appearing in all of its disguises, because you take these disguises as genuine and continue to buy into the promises that these disguises seem to carry. Sometimes the disguise is a friend, sometimes it is a job, sometimes this and sometimes that. Something always makes you hope again. Can you see that suffering and hope are inseparable?

So, in your opinion, one is actually better off feeling bad?

When you feel bad, there is the possibility of recognizing the underlying cause of your suffering. You yourself have made the impressive observation that people are only ready to take a step when the suffering has become unbearable, when suddenly all the usual strategies of denial no longer work. Disease shows up. A beloved one dies. A relationship is broken off. Catastrophic events do not actually create suffering but merely uncover it. They shake you out of the illusion that you are not already suffering. This is the greatest illusion people indulge in, and because of this illusion, they are not ready to wake up from suffering. Why should they? Suffering is a chain of sufferings and joys.

* * *

Much more serious than the fact that there is suffering is the fact that there is no recognition of suffering. This became very clear to me while I was in India, because in India, there even exists something like a devotion to suffering. But here in the West, where the dream has reached such a degree of prosperity and fulfillment of the survival instincts, the deception that you are not suffering is even stronger and more dangerous. Total recognition of suffering is the first and essential step towards bliss.

Once you have recognized suffering, the grace that my teacher, Gangaji, called your birthright is available to you. It is your birthright to liberate yourself from suffering. The question is not whether this right is available; the question is whether you are ready to accept it! Most people are not ready. They believe, "I am just fine, everything's quite okay, I sleep well, I have enough to eat, I have a partner, I have a job that is improving, everything's just wonderful after all." Everything really can be wonderful — for a period of time — but then the moment comes when you have to face the truth of suffering eye to eye. And this moment can be now. Then there is no longer any possibility of delaying the recognition of truth.

I thank my lucky stars that I was always aware of not being happy. As a small child, I experienced something like happiness for a while. But when adolescence hit, there was a dramatic phase like a fall, a relapse into hell, and the moment came when I was aware without any doubt that I had lost paradise, and no matter what I might do from there on out, no matter how well things might turn out, none of it would bring happiness again.

The recognition of suffering is not an ocean to stop and bathe in. It is a conscious and clear recognition, and out of this recognition, the longing for liberation grows. As Poonjaji said, "The total longing for liberation is in itself already free!"

* * *

What is your true priority? Usually, the inessential is given priority. The inessential is used as an excuse by the mind not to fight for liberation as if for your life. Who struggles that much for liberation? Here is a beautiful story:

Every day a student used to ask this same question: "How can I find God?" And every day, he received the same mysterious answer: "By longing."

" But I long for God with all my heart," replied the student. "Why, then, haven't I found him yet?"

One day, the Master accidentally took a bath in the river together with the student. He pushed the head of the man under water and held it there tight while the poor guy was trying desperately to break away.

The next day the Master started up a conversation: "Why were you fighting so much while I was holding your head under water? The student answered, "Because I was gasping for breath." The Master replied, "When you are granted the grace to struggle for God as much as you were struggling for breath, then you have found Him."

This is what I am saying. Usually, there is not a complete awareness of suffering. To avoid the awareness of suffering is a subtle kind of masochism. It's understandable to refrain from the self-inflicted suffering often advocated by the Church, which is the other polarity. Particularly here in the Christian tradition of the West, we are still trying to liberate ourselves from this collective trauma of Christianity, the religion of suffering.

When I speak of the awareness of suffering, I am not referring to any concept of you or someone else going through something painful for a certain period of time. It has nothing to do with time and space. It is about recognizing the defenses against the awareness of suffering. Continuing to look for pleasure in the illusion, to look for pleasure instead of joy, is ultimately the subtlest form of masochism. And it is not really about not experiencing any pleasure in the illusion. It is about recognizing the unfulfilled desire that drives the search.

Pleasure can be recognized as a manipulation, a defense against really seeing the hidden suffering. But once you recognize it, perhaps you will summon up the ruthlessness to cut through this age-old habit of attachment. Here is another story:

A Zen master asks his student to go to the lake near his house and fetch a cup of water for him. But as the student is standing at the banks of the lake with the empty cup to draw water, he suddenly sees in the distance a wonderfully beautiful young girl with long, blond hair. When their eyes meet, they fall immediately in love. She is the daughter of a farmer from a neighboring village and takes him with her to her family's farm. They marry and beget children. When the father dies, the student takes over the farm and he and his wife run it together. They spend many happy years together.

One year, at the beginning of fall when he is busy bringing in the harvest, a terrible storm suddenly blows in and a tidal wave floods the village. As the water rises higher and higher, he climbs onto the roof of his farm with his wife and children. His children are caught by the storm one by one and washed into the floods. So is his wife. Finally, desperate and sobbing, he is squatting on the gable of the house. All of those happy years are passing before his eyes when somebody taps him on the shoulder from behind. It is his teacher who then asks him, "What has taken you so long? I sent you out to fetch a cup of water from the lake."

* * *

Isn't life just a continuous play of changes? I still don't see it as an illusion.

At the very last, when you experience the fear of loosing life, you will see the illusion. Unfortunately, people live this illusion for lifetime after lifetime and notice the unreality of the illusion only the moment before they leave the body. First there is fear, and then there is the revelation that life was just an illusion. It is as much an illusion as a dream is an illusion. This life is just another kind of dream. There are day dreams and there are night dreams. This is a day dream.

It is not necessary to debate whether you are an illusion or not. There have been plenty of philosophical conversations about it. It's time to examine what your actual experience is. The notion of illusion points to the tendency to cling to what is dying. Everything is already dying. The body is already dying. It has been dying since the moment of its birth. See if you can access the fear of loosing everything. What remains when you loose everything—and you certainly will loose everything—is *that* which *is* always here this moment.

The Promise of Unfulfilled Desires

What we call suffering is like a roller coaster: When negative phenomena arise, we feel bad, and when positive phenomena arise, we feel good. Suffering has a wavy quality, a changing identification between the positive and the negative. The moment you identify with euphoric feelings, for instance if you have won a lottery prize, you are subconsciously already identifying with negative feelings, for example the fear of loss. At their core, every positive feeling contains a negative feeling, and every negative feeling contains a positive feeling.

There are certain phenomena or dream sequences that tempt you to leave the truth of yourself more than others do. You do not really leave the *Self*, it only appears to you like that. And if it appears to you like that, I can tell you, you do it voluntarily. There is this interplay between the forces interested in suffering and the forces interested in authentic and complete liberation. There seems to be such a strain and struggle, and frequently you cannot distinguish between the two forces. The problem is that the forces interested in suffering are frequently disguised as forces interested in happiness. If the forces interested in suffering were gross enough to always bring you suffering, quite obviously, you would say, "No, thank you," and reject them. But the exact difficulty is that these forces are capable of deception.

For instance, the forces of suffering can appear as deceptions by pretending to fulfill certain desires that you had hoped would be fulfilled. This roller coaster is maintained by more unfulfilled desires. It is the eternal duality, the eternal polarity, the eternal dichotomy that a desire that seems positive to you always has a negative core. I call this negative core a built-in, automatic igniter. It is a subconscious strategy of non-fulfillment, for desires are never fulfilled in exactly the same way or forever.

The truth is that you continually identify with phenomena and things to which you attach some kind of desire, no matter whether these things are inside or outside. If there are no unfulfilled desires, there is no identification. This organism is nothing but a body of desires. It is composed of the desires of the *thinking mind*. Now that you recognize you have this body of desires, what happens next? To be ready to face these false desires, you need absolute truthfulness, for it is not pleasurable to face these desires. It isn't necessarily pleasurable to admit that you have always only pretended to want to get rid of fear when in reality you have attached hidden desires to it. It isn't necessarily comfortable to admit with this kind of clarity that you have always pretended to want to get rid of guilt when in actuality you have attached hidden desires to it. But it is only unpleasant in the first moment, for as soon as you really see it, already this true *seeing* reveals the absurdity and falseness of unfulfilled desires, and there is then the possibility of understanding that this is not your true desire.

You hope for something that will never be fulfilled. Hope is never fulfilled. Every hope is an illusion. So your situation is hopeless but not serious. Right now, there is *That-Which-Is*, and right now, you can find *That-Which-Is* to be everything you have searched for. Hope, however, is always directed toward sometime in the future, a "sometime" that does not exist.

Are you aware of what it means that everything creating some form of suffering is solely held on to by attaching desires to it you were not ready to realize until now?

But sometimes it happens that my desires are fulfilled.

In the fulfillment of one desire, immediately another desire trails behind it. Let us assume you now occupy your attention with positive exercises, positive affirmations. You desire that within the next two months you will finally find the dream woman of your life. There are many teachings that tell you all you need do is desire it strongly enough, and it will be fulfilled. And actually, after two months it happens exactly as everybody said it would, but now let's wait for two more months. Without your even noticing, the fulfillment of one desire has already become the unfulfillment of the next higher desire. There has just been a shift to another level. This is how the infinite chains of unfulfilled desires work, doing nothing but shifting to another level once one desire out of the chain has been fulfilled. The whole of humanity is fooled by this game of unfulfilled desires. Only a few see through this game. It is an absolute fraud, it is the game of temptation, and you are continually cheated. You are cheated out of freedom. You are cheated out of the heart. You are cheated out of what you really *are*.

The moment an unfulfilled desire arises in consciousness, be vigilant. If you are very vigilant, and you explore the moment that you touch this desire, you will immediately recognize that it causes suffering. In reality, every unfulfilled desire is the desire for suffering. See how quickly suffering appears when you touch this desire. When you notice this, ask yourself if you still feel ready to touch these desires, if you are still ready to create suffering for yourself. It's as if the *thinking mind* has planted a seed of conflict that keeps you believing you don't have the right to be in complete peace. This is what it always amounts to: something or somebody seems to deny you the right to be in complete peace. There is nothing and nobody that keeps you away from it except yourself.

An unfulfilled desire is just a thought, having nothing to do with this moment. It comes from the past and is directed toward the future. The more vigilant you are, the sooner you will recognize that any expression of an unfulfilled desire necessarily leads to suffering. This can be surprising because the unfulfilled desire, after all, promises to relieve your suffering the moment it is fulfilled. Strangely, however, this fulfillment never occurs, in any case not completely and continually. Therefore, it is up to you and your determination as to whether or not you give up this desire or you keep it. Most people keep it, because they are not willing to accept that the desire does not reach its goal and never will.

* * *

Ultimately, it is all about finding out what your true desire is. If it is your desire to be loved, then it is more than probable your desire will never be fulfilled. You have to be very clear about this. If it is your desire to change the world, you also have to see that this desire will never be fulfilled. These desires are inessential.

The world is not changed by unfulfilled desires. It is not touched by them at all. It is merely the megalomania and the ignorance of a thought giving itself the power and pretending to be separate, to have free will, to act in separation from the One that keeps the world alive, that creates the world, that maintains and destroys the world, and does so in this moment. In this moment, the world is created, and in this moment, it is destroyed.

Notice this childish and obstinate clinging to unfulfilled desires. In reality, there still remains a little spark of hope. You still keep hiding a little stash, just in case. It is these little sparks of hope remaining stored somewhere that keep you from really looking closely and radically. A radical cut is required because like everyone else, you have the tendency to go on saving these little corners where the dust gathers, where you don't like to look closely, and where the attention can discreetly pass over. This is where the hidden reserves of suffering are kept. When you recognize clearly that the promise of these hidden reserves is a false promise, and if you have any self-respect, . . . well, draw your own conclusions. What kind of self-treatment is this when you keep pursuing something even when you know it causes suffering? Certainly, this is some kind of masochism.

* * *

What is karma?

Karma is what we call the film of life. In the film of life, the actions of seemingly separate individuals are like a wheel in time that is nourished by the past. The *thinking mind*, the creator of karma, is caught in this wheel, this labyrinth, this eternal chain of cause and effect where preconceived ideas and unfulfilled desires are followed in the search for fulfillment. Naturally, these desires are never fulfilled the way the *thinking mind* would like them to be, which gives rise to new unfulfilled desires. And each turn of the wheel in this search for personal satisfaction quite tangibly brings a certain amount of destructiveness through feelings like jealousy, anger, and pride, just to name a few.

When the *thinking mind* disappears, when it is completely recognized that the *thinking mind* is nothing but a thought that has no root, karma still continues like the natural momentum of an already flowing stream, or as Gangaji puts it, the momentum of an arrow that was shot a long time ago. The arrow that is this incarnation was shot a long time ago, and it takes its course. All the events that happen are in some way the consequences of past events that occurred during this arrow's flight.

You've certainly heard karma spoken of as being positive or negative. In the core of all karma is a natural and authentic desire for liberation. It's just that during the flight of this arrow the original and authentic desire for liberation has been continually discolored, falsified, and diverted into other desires, and in this way, access to the original desire for liberation has been lost.

The whole karmic process fundamentally consists of pursuing all the desires that disguise the one desire for freedom. First there is disappointment, then the renewal of the pursuit, then disappointment again and again until some point is reached where there is the possibility of opening once again to this original desire, this original longing, and a withdrawing from the chain of compulsive entanglements. This kind of withdrawal is not an act of the *thinking mind* but happens on its own through recognition, through surrender to your heart, for the heart is not touched by karma. Karma is a construct of the *thinking mind*.

Indolence, Fear, and Anger

Indolence is never ready to give everything. Giving everything is not within its horizon. Who is ready to give everything? Indolence is the desire to feel good rather than the desire to be free.

It seems as if a repeated shock is necessary to permanently wake up from indolence, especially if you have recognized that you don't need much in life, that you can be satisfied with what you have, and everything seems to be wonderful.

Indolence, otherwise known as laziness, is the most dangerous disguise of suffering because in this form, suffering is not obvious as suffering. The attachment to the relative bliss of laziness is not obvious. The truth is that this relative bliss is dependent on certain circumstances, on certain phenomena, and when these phenomena change, there won't be much bliss left either. But in the moment of pure indolence, one is not completely aware of it.

I can say that a repeated shock seems to be necessary to interrupt the landing in indolence. The shock is a kind of death that exposes what is not true.

Is it possible for me to create this shock myself?

No, the teacher will create the shock.

And life can be the teacher as well?

It is not known how the teacher will appear, as a person or as so-called circumstance, but it will appear.

* * *

How can I work on the indolence that separates my individual consciousness from its source?

Spiritual indolence is one of the deepest habits of the human mind. If we start from the "seeming" reality that indolence is in fact what separates you from the source, then I have to ask you, what do you *really* want?

In your case, it looks as if you fight against your indolence, that indolence is not what you want. The trick is that you pretend you want something else other than that, when, in fact, you *want* to rest in indolence and escape the discomfort of what I have called the "pain of awakening." The pain of awakening is insignificant. The compensation for it is the taste of this sweetness, of the divinity that is not hidden by any form. There is no question that truth is not the most convenient way. The most convenient way consists of falling asleep and devoting oneself to false knowledge of the mind, or directly cherishing sensual pleasures and taking this for paradise. This illusory paradise can appear for a while like true paradise, but it is transitory. Anything that is transitory will at some point turn around and show its other side, its evil side, its bad side, and possibly then you will recognize that clinging to it really does cause suffering.

It is especially difficult for those who seem to dwell on the sunny side of life. This very sunny side is what the human mind uses to numb the deep despair that drives it and seemingly bans despair from consciousness. If you are one of the few who have conscious access to the pain of separation and to the longing that rises out of this pain, then you are lucky.

To fight against indolence is useless. As long as you believe you have to fight indolence, you will pretend to fight against it, and this covers the fact that you are actually not willing to let it go.

Just be ready to go deeper. What is it you really want? What is your answer? You can only be completely honest with this question, for the moment you deny any latent desires, indolence remains. This trickles down to very practical areas of life. It is possible in a single moment to completely stop smoking cigarettes. The moment you simply recognize that it is not what you really want, that it doesn't support you and your search, it is over. It is possible to give up every harmful habit immediately in this second because you are the one who keeps the habit going.

You will have your reasons to keep the habit going. The mind is an extremely tricky charlatan. It can be very clever at pretending to fight against harmful habits that it has itself created, yet it is exactly this splitting by which the habits of mind are maintained. Instead, just recognize what is it you really want. Every fight within the *thinking mind* is a senseless fight that will not be won by either side. It is just shadow boxing between two "boxers" coming from the same source.

There is an antidote for indolence. For each of its tendencies the human mind also has a cure. Consequently, one could say, the strongest poison also contains the strongest antidote. When you explore a tendency you have recognized within yourself, for instance indolence, you know that this indolence is your enemy only as long as you fight against it. When you recognize that this tendency can also become your ally, you can then follow the tendency back to its source to see what it has to reveal. You can let indolence take your hand and show you where it leads you, which is to its other side, to its "shadow." It is this kind of self-investigation that will reveal the antidote not only for indolence but any other tendency of habit of the mind.

Indolence has a shadow just as everything else arising in your mind has a shadow or another side to it. No coin has just one side. When you recognize this, you can be aware of the shadow.

The shadow of indolence is also its cure. The shadow itself is *vigilance*. At first vigilance may seem to require effort simply because it doesn't correspond to your usual habits. It is not the habit of the human mind to be vigilant.

The truth is, however, that the moment you discover the truth of vigilance, you can use it as your ally. Every habit dissolves the moment the antidote, which is the habit's own shadow, is discovered and explored. It is exactly the same with all other tendencies as well. If, for instance, you have a tendency of doubt, this doubt has a shadow. Instead of seeing the doubt as a habit that has to be gotten rid of, look deeper to find its shadow, its polarity. The doubt *has* to have a shadow. The polarity of doubt is what we call faith. All that is required is to look closely. When you do, the tendency is already dissolving.

* * *

I am afraid of life. I try to shake off the fear, but it keeps reappearing.

Fear is your ally. Fear is your teacher and can lead you to liberation. It is an essential ally, and it is commonly misunderstood. Normally, fear is fought against and not listened to. There is fear of fear. Fear is not usually recognized and very few people have ever truly experienced it.

Fear leads you to the essential. Fears relating to something concrete are *inessential*. If you perceive fears that relate to concrete situations or things, then you can explore these fears and let yourself be led deeper. Other fears are always hidden behind them. Ultimately, all fears melt together into one. This one fear, if it can be named, is ultimately the fear of death, the fear of emptiness, but it is still attached to a mental concept. In order to detach it from any concept, you must pursue this fear to its core. Fear can only be an ally leading to Being if you are ready to detach it from any mental concept.

Fear is not about what it is seems to be about, even though it may seem to be evoked by certain people or certain situations. Those fears only point to something deeper. But the possibility of ultimately detaching fear from any concept and directing the attention to the core of fear is contradictory to the usual direction attention goes when fear appears. Usually you direct the attention away from fear, i.e., toward thoughts or toward the body or toward something on the outside. In other words, every thought about fear is a lost thought leading away from the essential. It is possible to follow fear into the depths where it actually wants to lead you.

Don't try to take any action against fear. It is no use. It cannot be overcome. There is this idea, perhaps even a spiritual idea, that fear has to be overcome. I would assert that it is not possible to overcome fear. Every attempt to overcome fear leads to fixating it again in the subconscious so that it never dissolves, even if through this attempt, it seems to be gone at first, offering the illusion it can be brought under control. The same is true for confronting fear. Fear will never dissolve by being confronted. There is no possibility of dissolving fear by any kind of doing. The problem, exclusively, is the one who is doing.

Deep down, every identification of a human being is driven by fear. Whether the person is aware of it or not doesn't matter at all. Whenever someone adopts a practice of meditation, at some point fear will inevitably appear to an extreme degree. It is at this point that you can make the conscious choice to recognize it as an ally or to treat it further as an enemy, which is what people normally do. Because fear is uncomfortable, it has to be dealt with or somehow treated. Ultimately, every attempt to treat fear is a defense against it, an attempt to somehow dissipate it. There is only one possibility of dealing with fear and that is to give up every dealing, every occupation, every therapy, every doing—to give up *everything*. The moment that fear arises completely and nakedly in consciousness, there is the possibility of seeing it for what it is—a channel, a funnel that leads deeper and opens up something hidden beneath it.

For certain people, it may be important to treat fear in the beginning, because initially a certain minimum of relaxation may be needed in order to go deeper into the fear. This can be difficult when fear, once it appears, seems to get out of control, as in some cases with a phobia, although this basically just points to an unreadiness to explore reality. All phenomena arising around fear and taken for fear itself are quite obviously unreal. However, if somebody sees ghosts and somehow takes these ghosts to be real in a very identified way, it may be appropriate at first to find a certain release from this identification and only then to go deeper. But those who are truly ready to directly experience the *essence* of fear have to recognize that every doing, every thinking, every shrinking back, every therapy, is only an attempt at dissipating the fear. The most direct way, I would even go as far as to say the *only* way to experience reality directly, is *non-doing*. And it is this non-doing that appears to be so infinitely difficult to most people when in truth, it is simpler than simple.

* * *

Fear cannot be removed from the world by logical, rational thought. In satsang, we no longer have to be concerned with the rational. Besides, the mind pretending to be rational is totally irrational. The motivations of this rational mental structure are totally irrational. Fear cannot be sorted out by thought.

Fear has its origin in the experience of separation from the divine. The principal idea on which fear is based is the idea that the self can be destroyed. Fear arises out of the "idea" of *nothingness*. It is, in fact, not possible for the mind to touch this *nothingness* by thought. Yet the mind takes its idea of nothingness for nothingness itself. And this idea of nothingness is directly attached and interlaced with the fear that the self can be destroyed. It can be there either as a conscious idea or perhaps as a sensation, and this may vary. It is a concept of *not-being*. What the mind associates with death is always what it associates with *nothingness*. As the mind takes the "appearance" of life for life itself, it believes that life can be killed. But life cannot be killed.

* * *

There seem to be different forms of fear. The fear that I spontaneously experience as a reaction to physical threat does not seem to be the same as the fear that is potentially always lurking about.

There is fear and there is fear. There is fear as "Rembrandt" and there is fear as a "copy of Rembrandt." Everything that spontaneously, unpredictably, and uncontrollably arises from this moment is "Rembrandt." Every inner manifestation that is tainted by ideas of the past is a copy. Everything created by an I- idea is a falsification.

If you cross the street and someone suddenly approaches you drawing a weapon, you are afraid. In this instance, fear is a spontaneous, direct and natural reaction. That is "Rembrandt." That is life. That is authentic. That is what is played in the dream.

But this kind of fear is not the fear you suffer from. The fear you suffer from, which is this nagging fear that you say "lurks about," has yet to be truly recognized. It arises from the catacombs of the graveyard. The catacombs of the graveyard are what I call the "karmic story," what I call the past, what I call ignorance. A distinction has to be made here, a separation, a disentanglement of the feeling of fear from the past idea of fear so that the fear can be experienced directly. When fear is experienced directly, then the seeming interlacing of the feeling of fear with the past is cancelled out, and it becomes possible to fall deeper. Feelings are like tunnels that lead you deeper into the experience of Self.

Anger can be another powerful tunnel if you are willing to experience it directly all the way to its core. However, if you experience resistance to anger, then this is no longer anger but already some kind of an interlacing. Resistance is a lukewarm copy of the power of the "original," the fire of anger itself. This fire is not directed against anything. Only thoughts direct it against something. If you don't follow the anger with thoughts, the fire takes its own direction.

Anger is not a thought. As soon as you believe that anger is directed against something, you are dwelling in thoughts and not purely experiencing the anger. This happens to you again and again. You keep falling into this same trap. Anger is not resistance at all. Anger is energy. Anger is pure shakti, pure energy, but then all the mental justifications arise as to "why" you are angry. Then anger is given meaning, and you get caught in the meaning instead of simply recognizing that anger is anger, rage is rage. Meanings are insignificant. As soon as you give importance to any meaning, you are no longer in reality, because a meaning can only be given according to a limited level of understanding. This means that there is no ultimate answer to your question. If you want an answer, here is the answer given in the Zen tradition: It doesn't mean *anything*.

Suffering is a Delusion

The Buddha's approach was this: Recognize the origin of suffering and you attain liberation. In the last hundred years since Freud, therapy seems to have proceeded in a similar way. People are suffering, so they go to the therapist wanting to find the origin of their suffering. Both the Buddha's approach and Freud's approach obviously deal with the mind. Can you say something about how the mind and suffering are interconnected?

There are different avenues of approaching suffering, depending on the level of understanding of the seeker. Therapy primarily starts out from the idea that suffering has come into existence through the past. I try to guide people to experience the exact moment in which suffering arises. To be more precise, suffering doesn't just happen. It is an actively initiated process. Suffering is attachment or clinging. The ego is a synonym for either attachment or clinging. You could just as well call the notion of clinging the notion of relationship.

Gangaji said that suffering is the relationship with pain. Most people believe that pain itself is suffering, but pain is not suffering. Suffering consists of an assumed "I" who has a personal relationship with pain, who clings to or rejects pain and therefore suffers. In the total merging with pain, suffering is no more.

Suffering, as such, is a delusion. In reality, there is no suffering. Whether the body is healthy or not, whether there is emotional pain or joy, it does not matter, and it does not touch the latent bliss. By this, I do not mean that pain is as agreeable as joy or that physical disease is as agreeable as physical health. This is simply not the point. People confuse disease with suffering. It is possible, in fact, to be happy with a very sick body.

Does suffering happen exclusively in the mind?

Yes. Suffering happens exclusively in the *thinking mind*. In *No-Mind*, suffering does not exist.

Whatever keeps suffering and the clinging to suffering in motion is a mechanism in the mind that pushes the awareness of suffering into the subconscious. This mechanism can be called indolence, literally meaning: intolerance towards the experience of pain. No one would be ready, in fact, to suffer in total consciousness. Consequently, as I stated before, suffering itself is not the problem. The problem is the lack of conscious awareness about the suffering, the denial of suffering, and the ensuing numbness.

This indicates that suffering is not acute depression or mourning but something seated much deeper than that — the fact that I do not know who I am.

Yes. As long as there is an "I" who blindly identifies with being an individual separate from oneness, there is suffering.

So, what is normally described as happiness is just another form of suffering?

Yes, what is normally described as happiness is just another form of suffering.

Suffering can be considered either a friend or an enemy. In the spiritual process of awakening, suffering becomes more and more accepted as an ally, as a transmitter of recognition and not as something that has to be destroyed.

* * *

How could I be happy if, as you propose, I were to lose everything, even my feelings?

By "lose everything," I mean not to take ownership of your feelings. The experience of loss is painful, but when you lose *everything,* do you have the experience of *really* having lost something? Do you feel the tension that arises from the fear of losing something? Do you realize how much this tension seems to take possession of you as long as you are afraid of losing things?

How about losing everything in one moment, *in this moment*? How about being willing to experience losing everything and then seeing whether you have *really* lost everything? If you lose the body, you will lose the body anyway, so why not *now*? If you lose feelings, well, you continually lose feelings anyway, so why not *now*? If you lose thoughts, you continually have the experience of losing thoughts anyway, so why not *now*?

Your problem consists of claiming these things for yourself, of taking ownership of things that do not belong to you. When you take ownership of things that don't belong to you, then you suffer because you believe you have to hold on to them. You are free when all of these things appear in you and disappear in you without your having to take ownership of them. The problem is not that these negative feelings arise in you, they will always arise, sometime, somehow, but you don't have to possess them. You need not pretend that they are *your* feelings or *your* body or *your* thoughts. How do you know this anyway? Do you see how naturally you simply claim that some kinds of phenomena are yours? It is like you willingly take possession of suffering and then complain about it. Something arising in consciousness is not naturally yours. Imagine that nothing is yours.

It is difficult to imagine this.

You can in this moment experience what it is like when you are simply still and don't touch any story, any emotion. Then you can relax.

And if they come back after that?

Let them come back, but let them alone. It is quite arbitrary how you make certain feelings *your* feelings and emphatically reject others. When you recognize that nothing is truly *yours*, it makes it a very simple matter.

Some kinds of phenomena that arise are declared arrogantly to be "me," and no one has ever questioned it. This is actually the meaning of arrogance. Arrogance means to claim something as yours that doesn't belong to you. And nothing truly belongs to you.

What remains when you lose everything?

Then there is peace.

Yes. Peace always remains with you, and the question is simply whether you know how to appreciate it. This peace is always there. You need no feeling to experience this peace, you need no thought, and neither do you need a body.

* * *

When you try to possess something that is obviously impermanent, you have to live in the tension of the possibility of losing it. Recognize that everything you consider a part of yourself, but which is not permanent, creates the tension of having to hold on to it. Whether it appears as a recognition or as a great range of different feelings, images, or thoughts, it doesn't matter. It is always only about one thing, and that is death. And obviously, every *thing* dies.

* * *

You never suffer from the object you are resisting, whether it is pain or fear or objects in the outside world. You suffer from the resistance itself.

Resistance itself is suffering?

Yes. The mind, with its inaccurate view, equates suffering with negative states. Usually, the equation is that "suffering equals pain," and as soon as you sense pain coming you draw back, you resist it. In that moment, what you don't realize is that the pain is not the cause of your suffering.

I am certain there must have been some moment in which you were open, you felt protected, you felt trust, and you experienced that suffering was over the instant you surrendered to pain. Strangely, though, there is some kind of disturbance in the mind's ability to learn. You do not suffer the moment you surrender to pain or whatever else you are trying to avoid. Rather, the suffering arises when there is some kind of resistance, some kind of withdrawal or turning away. At this moment, there is a distancing or separation. What if you don't distance yourself from anything? The truth is that you are not distant from anything. All distancing is artificial.

Fear of fear is a typical form of distancing, and resistance is another form of distancing. When you are simply with what is shown to you in this moment, watch carefully what happens. By going into resistance, you are in relationship with pain. The moment you surrender, there is no longer any relationship because relationship can only exist if there are two. Therefore, I keep saying that every form of relationship has to be given up. With whomever or whatever you believe you have a relationship, give it up.

I don't understand. Why is it no longer a relationship when I surrender?

The moment you surrender to pain, there is no separation between you and the pain. Your fear says that when every control and every resistance is given up, you will drown. But is this really your experience? Satsang is all about distinguishing your simple and direct experience from some idea of experience. As long as you can't distinguish between your direct experience and your ideas, you get lost in the labyrinth of the mind. Be aware of the tendency to go into some kind of distance or avoidance, and have the courage to be with what is here, no matter what it is. Nothing has to be avoided, and nothing has to be held on to. Even when a feeling of bliss arises, this feeling does not need to be held on to.

And what about emotional pain?

As to emotional pain, I can only tell you that it is absolutely not natural for certain emotional states to last for a long time. My experience is that emotions, or even more accurately, feelings, appear and disappear within a very short time as long as there isn't any attachment to some I-thought. Feelings only last for long periods because they are kept alive artificially, held on to artificially, or dramatized and sentimentalized in some way.

There are many ways to somehow manipulate an authentic, spontaneous feeling so that it stays, for instance when the mind suppresses a feeling under the pretense of protecting you. But this doesn't work, does it? If you will honestly examine this, you will see that any suppression of an emotion or any dramatization of an emotion never results in your escaping something or something being released. Suppression of emotion never results in liberation. Liberation is only possible in complete non-doing, which means giving up every doing.

The mind knows very subtle forms of doing. For instance, it disguises doing with a cloak of passivity, and this is another form of indolence. Indolence is also doing. Freedom is about giving up all of these very subtle forms of doing and totally facing what *is*—beyond any thought, beyond any idea, beyond any concept, without any past, without any future.

The suffering of emotionally difficult states does not arise out of the experience itself. The experience of pain is not suffering. What is suffering? It is what you *make* of the pain. Whatever you think brings about suffering, and unhappiness is your never ending story. And where does the story come from? It comes from somewhere other than from *life*.

Are you saying that the story that creates pain is actually dead?

Yes, every story is dead. As long as the mind, for whatever reasons, is not ready to let go of these dead stories, they are slipped over the experience of the moment, and then mixed up, and then it is the story, which is your relationship to whatever is arising in the moment, that creates suffering. The story is all of the concepts, ideas, and memories that have grown up around the pain and by which the pain is armored.

Perhaps you work with seriously ill people. When you are ready to be with the pain and not with the concepts around the pain—not only for yourself but for everyone else—when you are ready to one hundred percent give up all distancing and be with this pain without giving it any meaning, then compassion is possible. Everything, especially feelings, has to be detached from every concept, every story, and every pseudo-meaning given to them. They don't have any meaning. The feeling itself is not dead. Meaning kills it. No feeling has any meaning. When you give up the distance you create by putting some concept between yourself and the feeling, then there is no longer any question and there is no longer any suffering. It is very simple.

Then are you suggesting to give up feelings in order to attain liberation?

No. It is not about giving up feelings. I am talking about giving up the *meaning* that the mind gives to feelings. The preference for *mental* thought and giving it meaning is certainly the trauma of the male, and the preference for *emotional* thought and giving it meaning is certainly the trauma of the female. Liberation is about letting go of both, as they are misunderstandings.

* * *

In India, I experienced a deep feeling of happiness and bliss, but now it is gone. How can I get it back?

Many people are interested in attaining special states, keeping special states, or repeating special states, whether they are states of happiness or states of pain. Some people are keen on attaining states of pain again and again. However, I have observed with many spiritual seekers that the attachment to pain switches and becomes an attachment to an idea of the feeling of happiness. It is possible to give up interest in any state.

Ultimately, it doesn't matter which states appear. *The problem is your relationship with these states,* and all of the mental activity such as, "I like this state, I dislike that state, I want to get rid of this state," and so on. Then you try, via your memories, to somehow regain a state that of course is inevitably lost. No state can be regained. Even though states may seem very similar, the same state will never appear again. There are yogis who have themselves buried for three years and they remain in a state of *samadhi*, of deep, blissful meditation until they are unburied, and then the state is finished. Every state passes. It is not about attaining some particular state, about going to a master, attaining a feeling of bliss, and then trying to somehow preserve this feeling of bliss. The attachment to any state is a problem, whether it is a positive state or a negative state.

I continue to meet many seekers who go to spiritual masters and then cling very strongly to states of bliss. But the moment the form of the master dies (the master does not die but the form does), the states of bliss are finished because they are transitory.

All except one state.

Yes. The eternal state.

Whatever state you experience, don't touch it, even if the tendency arises of wanting or do something with them because somebody classified them as undesirable. If you experience anger, so what? It doesn't matter.

The mind that sets out on a spiritual search can just shift suffering to another level by wrapping it in spiritual concepts. For instance, "I must not feel jealousy; it does not indicate a high spiritual level." "I must not experience anger; it does not correspond to holiness," etc. These concepts are the real problem. Anger and jealousy are not the problem. The problem is your relationship to them.

What do you think would happen if you gave up all your preferences and dislikes? All preferences and dislikes are developed out of arbitrary conditioning. They are not important. It is not essential whether somebody thinks something is beautiful or ugly. The only thing essential about it is that the one who is identified with this evaluation suffers from it. The mind always pretends that evaluations have some kind of reality — "I think this is right. I think that is wrong." What are these standards of right and wrong based upon?

On comparison.

Yes, and according to what criteria are things compared? There can only be comparison if this moment is compared to something in the past. The habit of mind is to get into relationship with the past and to compare. There is a belief that if every standard breaks down, chaos will ensue. Actually, this desperate attempt to create an identity by applying a standard is responsible for all suffering. What if standards no longer exist? What if there is no longer the possibility or necessity of evaluating? You are not even aware of *who* is evaluating. The mind definitely creates convincing mental concepts, but where do these concepts come from and what are they based upon?

* * *

Hate is something I don't allow myself to feel, and the other day I caught myself blocking it. What do I do with these strong feelings? And what about the joys of love and passion and closeness?

For you, it is about giving up your strong identifications with emotional states. When you are ready to give up your relationship with feelings, then the paradox is revealed that love and passion for life can arise out of this space without your having the desire for it.

Hate is not an authentic feeling. What I call hate is actually anger with a story wrapped around it that somehow dramatizes and inflates it. When you liberate hate from the story, which is ultimately always inessential, when you penetrate to the feeling itself, then you find that anger is nothing but energy. You don't have to do anything with anger. Rather than liberating yourself from anger, it can be helpful to think of it as liberating anger from the story. In other words, the story is not interesting. The "why" of the hate is ultimately insignificant. It is just one story among many stories, and the *thinking mind* tells a lot of stories. It will tell you anything. All of these emotions, however strong, are ultimately of no importance. You can take them to therapy, if you want to, you can try curing them, and to a certain degree, you will feel relieved. This can be temporarily helpful if someone is not ready to penetrate directly to the truth that every story is ultimately inessential. You give an importance to this feeling that it does not have, because you give importance to the relationship with feelings, and it doesn't have any importance.

Feelings are not life itself. Feelings are ultimately as inessential as thoughts. They come and they go. It is not about getting rid of feelings. It is okay if they come and it is okay if they don't come. Feelings just aren't essential. Satsang is about getting to the essential, the ultimate, and it is deeper than feelings and thoughts. Liberation cannot be experienced through thinking. Just be still, and most of all, be absolutely vigilant.

As I said before, true freedom is about giving up the relationship with anything and everything. It is even about giving up your relationship with life, because what you have taken for life until now is not life, it is just images of life. And everybody takes images of life for life itself. The body is not life, feelings are not life, and thoughts are not life. They arise *out of* life and are *in* life. Find out what is permanent and cannot be lost. Don't waste time relating with transitory and impermanent matters. This only makes you unhappy.

*   *   *

*Why is it that one experiences this greater unity, this oneness
with oneself much more when out amongst nature, or when
experiencing a deep connection with someone, or sometimes in
moments of great grief? And why, in daily work, do I have the
impression of moving away from mySelf?*

These distinctions are an illusion. What you take for
"I" when you believe you are moving away from *yourSelf* is
not you. For instance, when you *fully* surrender to the
experience of deep grief, it feels as if you *are* the core of this
grief. Suddenly, you feel very close with yourself. The truth
is you never move away from yourself, and since you
never move away, you never come closer either. You are
always what you are. You are *Consciousness*. Give up your
attachment to images and feelings. Give up your
attachment to grief.

Grief is a deep feeling that seems relatively nearer to
you than most other phenomena, yes, but grief is not *you*.
Realize yourself as the core of Being and every idea of
distance from yourself, of more or less intimacy with
yourself, will dissolve. Basically it doesn't matter where
*Darshan** takes place, whether it is in a beautiful, natural
setting or not. I would actually like just once to hold it in a
garbage dump so that the mind is ready to let go of all
attachments to what Satsang is, for in reality Darshan in a
garbage dump is exactly the same as Darshan anywhere
else. What is there is exactly *That* which is *here*. But you
could immediately misunderstand it again and begin
frequenting garbage dumps in an enforced way. Always
the mind has a tendency to fall into the opposite polarity.

What I am speaking of is actually the middle path. In
Buddhism, one speaks of this "Middle Path" that cuts
through the compulsion to fall into one side of the polarity
and then into the other. If you believe, "In virgin nature I

feel at home," this is still just a reflection of beauty and not beauty itself. In the moment that you make this judgment, without even noticing it you give rise to all the interpretations of where you are *not* at home—"I am at home here, but I am not at home there." "In the countryside I am at home, but in the city I am not at home." "In Germany I am at home, but in the United States I am not at home." Endless chains of comparisons between ideas are continually carried out as to where you are at home and where you are not.

The truth is you are at home everywhere. Everywhere where you *are*.

* * *

I often feel "high as a kite" and then once again "down in the dumps."

You give too much significance to your feelings. Sometimes the sun shines, and sometimes there is rain. So what? Ultimately it is not important whether the sun shines or it rains. In truth the sun shines all the time anyway. When you give up your deep attachment and preference for sunshine, then it is all just "weather." The bliss that I talk about has nothing to do with either "bad weather" or "sunshine." It is *That* from which all weather originates, that is to say, the sky.

Let the weather be the weather. It doesn't matter whether there is grief or rage, laughing or no laughing, feeling or no feeling. Those are not essential. You need not have any idea about what kind of feeling should be there and what kind shouldn't. What use is that? In any event, you know that the weather forecast only proves correct in a limited way, and this goes for the outside as well as the inside.

But I have a problem accepting all of the changing feelings in the same way that I can accept the weather.

When you say you have a problem giving up preferences and dislikes, recognize what they do to you. By this, you are saying, "I have a problem giving up suffering." The real mystery is that people want to give up everything else possible except suffering. When you give up suffering, the only thing you really lose is suffering. You have to be ready to lose it. And preferences are just a disguise for suffering. Fixated preferences and dislikes are disguises for suffering. As you may have already observed, preferences always want something different from what is. If you want something different from what *is*, you believe yourself to be separate from what *is*.

Strong preferences for certain weather situations have to do with identifying with the weather. You believe that when you experience joy, you are okay, but when you experience grief, you are not okay. When you feel good, you are okay, but when you feel small and weak, when you experience something you don't like, then you are not okay." Why do you define yourself according to the weather? Give this up! It is not your task to judge whatever experience appears in this moment. When you don't have to judge any longer, the experience of this moment can be quite authentic, and then it disappears again. The weather is relative. It changes. Find out what doesn't change.

Everything that appears is good, as the true nature of all things is good. Grief is also good. Just for once be aware of how you continually judge and interpret *what is* by labeling it right or wrong. This is a trance. People have even come to tell me how to give Satsang. Radically recognize the perfection of that which is in this moment, and be with it. You don't owe an explanation to anybody if there is sadness or anger. Sadness is just here, and then it leaves again. Next, something else is here, and then it leaves again. You don't owe any explanation. Be genuinely with whatever is here. Be with it without making a story out of it.

Do you see how simple it is? Do you see how difficult it is when there is continually something not okay? Then it has to be hidden, compensated, or altered so that it looks different, and then you have to feel guilty for it. It has to be judged, controlled, and manipulated, and then others have to be manipulated. It is an endless chain.

* * *

I have experienced a kind of state in which I am somehow in harmony with what happens, with all the ups and downs, and then at some point it changes. I don't notice it immediately when it changes, I just notice at some point I become lifeless, everything feels wrong, and I feel caught in the spider's web. I am not aware of the point where the flow of being shifts into suffering.

Are you aware of your judgments? If something is alive, it is right, and if something is lifeless, it is wrong? Feeling alive and feeling lifeless are part of duality. If there is a moment of lifelessness, so what? Lifelessness is your interpretation of a certain quality of experience. This quality of experience is not a problem. The problem is that the *thinking mind* keeps trying to cling to one of the polarities and excludes negativity. If you give up excluding negativity and allow it, negativity is a whole different experience.

The feeling of lifelessness does not create suffering. The suffering is your whole story behind it, the fear of ultimately dying in this lifelessness, of not existing, of loosing yourself, of dissolving. The suffering is not the original phenomenon of seeming lifelessness, which is at the most uncomfortable, but your whole drama around it. The tendencies of the past keep reappearing, and there is no possibility and no necessity of overcoming them. Let there be lifelessness. Remain still in the lifelessness, and give up the drama behind it. Allow lifelessness. Receive lifelessness also. Lifelessness is not separate from life.

Actually, there is no such thing as lifelessness. This is the confusion behind your question. The deep belief is that you exist when you feel alive. When there is lifelessness, you are afraid of not existing, afraid of loosing yourself, afraid of dying in this lifelessness. Be aware of this confusion between liveliness and life. Liveliness is life and lifelessness is also life. Everything is life. Death happens in life. Life is not destroyed, and neither is it your experience that life is destroyed. That you dissolve in this feeling of lifelessness and cease existing is not your actual experience. The mind looks for certain phenomena in order to suffer from them. It makes use also of this feeling of lifelessness. Let lifelessness pass and let liveliness pass too. The more you cling to liveliness, the more you will push away lifelessness, and vice versa. Many people are subject to this deception. It is a misunderstanding cultivated by many therapies that promote attaining and keeping such states. Any state happens in duality and is transient. How about giving up the attachment to liveliness and the attachment to lifelessness? What happens then?

Then everything is okay.

Who says that it is okay? Only somebody starting out from the idea that it might not be okay would affirm that it is okay. It is not okay, and it is not, not okay either. Experience *That-Which-Is* directly. There is equanimity in the experience of what *is*. Extraordinary experience — good, welcome it. Ordinary experience — also good, welcome it. Who knows what experience you will have in the next moment? Nobody knows. This kind of liveliness is genuine. It is not in polarity with lifelessness but arises fresh and spontaneously out of the true Self before anyone has a chance to say something about it.

The Desire for Liberation

You often talk about the one true desire. What is this true desire, this one desire among all desires?

The true and only desire of a human being is to be free, to be happy, to be at peace. It is the desire to be free of any limitation and to melt into one's true source, to return to the source from which the *thinking mind* seems to have separated. Not only when the body dies, but *now*. It is possible to recognize the origin of yourself *now*! But to recognize it, you must really have the desire for it. There is nobody, least of all God, to refuse your ultimate and absolute desire. Nobody would refuse you this desire because it is your birthright that this desire be fulfilled. Anyway, there has never been anyone to refuse you a desire. The reason this illusion of unfulfilled desires appears the way it does is because you are not aware of your hidden desires. That is all.

* * *

How do I get the recognition of "Now"? It always seems to me that there must be a path leading there, even though everybody says there is no path.

You have to ask yourself what it is you really want. To intellectually understand that everything you experience as reality, past and future, is an illusion, is of no use to you.

Everything that happens to you and that you call your life is an expression of your subconscious desires and comes into existence because your attention is directed towards it. The problem is that hardly anyone knows what he or she really wants. What is your deepest desire? As long as you are not ready to contact your deepest desire, as long as you are not ready to experience it directly without knowing what it really is or filtering it through your spiritual concepts, you will fall victim to the temptation of other desires, desires that will ultimately create some form of suffering.

My teacher, Gangaji, has described how she passed through different layers of these desires. There was the desire for a child and the belief that the child would make her happy. Many years later, it became apparent that wasn't it. Then the desire appeared to have a career as a healer and an acupuncturist. Everything went perfectly, and it again required some time until she really understood that this wasn't it either. And finally she came to the point of understanding that everything she had tried until then was ultimately futile, that ultimately she had not attained this total fulfillment she had originally longed for. This was the moment she inwardly let go of everything and knew that she could not carry on like this, that she needed a teacher. A teacher is nothing but a reflection of your own heart.

The past cannot be released as long as you are not aware of the hidden and partly infantile desires of the past. Perhaps you still carry the desire that your father will finally love you or finally apologize to you. There are infinite facets of desires continuously maintained on a hardly perceptible emotional level.

But where does all this lead you? Obviously, you must have *one* final desire, and you must have some consciousness about this desire, otherwise you would not have come here tonight. You could just as well have gone to the movies instead. Ask yourself, What do I really want? This question leads you deeper.

I want to come home.

Yes, to come home. What is your home? Your home is *Here.* It is not in the past. It is not in the future. It is not in the present. It is *Here.* It is not outside. It is not inside. It is *Here.* As soon as you try to understand, you are no longer *Here.* As soon as you make any effort to be here, you are no longer *Here.* You are *already* here. You can do nothing about it. Rather, it is about giving up what you continuously try to do in order not to be *Here.*

* * *

Every identification you burden yourself with has a firm hold on your longing to be free. Everything you have made part of *your* life is a burden on your freedom. Why have you burdened yourself with identifications? Because you have certain motivations for it. In other words, you have a certain desire for it because you want something from it. As long as you want something from it, you lose the energy for wanting freedom. It is as if your whole energy, your will, the true will of the Self, has split and dispersed into all directions on the most diverse levels. To become one with one's core, you must get this true will back again.

Direct this longing for freedom toward that which cannot be lost, that which is unknown, that which you don't understand, and to which you can only surrender. I can assure you that there is no danger, no possibility of anything going wrong. That life can be wrong is also just one of the many commentaries made by fear; that God does the wrong things at the wrong time, that God doesn't take care of you, that God doesn't like you, and so on. There is no possibility of anything going wrong. Just let the mind continue to relax.

The thought, "I want to be free," is absolutely rare. Most people don't have any interest in it. When this thought becomes more powerful than everything else you experience, more powerful than any other thought, more powerful than any make-believe reality of your life, when this thought seizes all the power and becomes a longing, then, as Poonjaji expressed it, this thought is already freedom itself.

* * *

For twenty years I have been regularly doing different kinds of spiritual practice, but I have not yet attained that final fulfillment of which you speak.

The question is always one of motivation. What is it that you want? What percentage of your attention goes toward nourishing your desire for liberation? This desire must be completely uncovered and that means one hundred percent. Not by a superhuman effort, but simply by uncovering your true desire and the absolute readiness to tell the truth to yourself. If there are any desires left that you would like to follow, that are more important to you, go after them. Do it, live it if you want to, but do not play this fifty percent game, this pretense of being interested in spirituality on the one hand but on the other hand not really. If there is still the desire to experience something you have forbidden yourself up until now, just do it. There is no problem with this. On the contrary, by carrying it around and not living it, it will just become more solid in the subconscious and not open up the view on what you really want. It often has to be experienced first that the fulfillment of unfulfilled desires does not lead to lasting fulfillment, to liberation, and only then is the mind ready to see that what it thought would fulfill you wasn't it.

There is such a pretense of holiness in the mind, such a pretense of holiness among spiritual seekers who fool themselves into thinking they are ready, rather than actually facing their latent unfulfilled desires. If there are desires, acknowledge them, live them fully for one moment and then just check to see whether it was what you really wanted or not. It is of no use to just try to be spiritually correct and desire what the teacher desires, i.e., that you search for liberation, because then liberation remains only a concept. The desire for freedom *must* come from your own self out of the willingness to ask yourself what it is you finally want deep down in your heart. This *true* desire is impersonal. It is free.

When I ask myself what I really want, I come to a point where I experience a haunting longing and nothing else.

Are you aware of this longing now?

Yes, and it is so big, it feels like it takes over my whole being

Good. Do nothing with this longing. Just be with it. This longing is like a vacuum, taking in all ignorance, all suffering, and all concepts. Ultimately, this longing will suck in the whole world, and all that remains is the heart itself. You need not do anything to support this longing. You need not do anything to maintain it. Just give up doing whatever takes your attention back into other unfulfilled needs. All doing, which you will be able to easily ascertain, takes you away from directly experiencing the longing. Stop everything that takes you away from it. Just be with it, nothing else, and witness what happens. It is very simple. The longing consumes your thoughts. It consumes everything.

* * *

Can the retreat of consciousness from the outside world to the inside also be a purely selfish process having nothing to do with genuine, ultimate readiness?

It is very possible that directing the attention inward is motivated by intentions that have nothing to do with the true readiness for self-liberation, motivations that are based primarily on the need to alleviate suffering. I would say this is initially the main intention of one hundred percent of spiritual seekers. However, in most cases, the mind inevitably lands on varied and subtle levels of indolence, because indolence is confused with the absence of suffering. The *thinking mind* can even try to co-opt transient feelings of bliss in order to land there because it is still not ready to be completely finished with suffering. Freedom is not really about alleviating suffering but about giving up, totally.

The *thinking mind* has a tendency to be satisfied with certain relative results. There are those who compromise throughout their whole lives just to attain some alleviation from suffering, and there are those who are totally radical and ready to give up everything and no longer compromise anything. Those are the people who want *everything*. For to want enlightenment, to want total self-liberation, you obviously have to want *everything*. You must not be satisfied with just a little. But the mind has a tendency of being satisfied with a little because the mind is itself a deficiency syndrome. It functions out of deficiency, and anything functioning out of a deficiency only attains more deficiency. Even if, through certain workshops dealing with positive thinking, the mind pretends to develop a temporary feeling of abundance, it will ultimately remain rooted in a deep identification with deficiency.

There is an unknown, primordial source of divine energy that feeds the *thinking mind*, and for unknown reasons it can happen that the primordial energy called shakti breaks through this deficiency syndrome. Then there can be the readiness to really give up everything. Or seen from another perspective, there can be the will to have everything, but not the way people would normally imagine in the sense of a lot of money or the best partner, etc. I'm speaking of everything in the sense of giving up suffering. To have *everything* is Being.

You cannot truthfully express the desire to be free as long as you are not totally aware of the shadow or the adversary of this desire, i.e., the desire not to be free. When the desire to be free finally appears as the only true desire in total awareness, when attention and energy are no longer split off from this desire, then this desire is freedom itself. Before that, a part of the attention is directed at the desire to be free and another part is always split off and directed at the unconscious desire not to be free. That is to say, you are sleeping. You are walking around holding your eyes closed, holding your ears closed, holding your mouth closed. This is called "unconsciousness." If you didn't actively hold your eyes, your ears, and your mouth closed, there would be no unconsciousness.

Are you aware of the desire not to be free?

I can sense its existence.

Yes, this is the moment when it starts emerging from the unconscious. This is the moment when you start liberating yourself from the shadow and thereby setting free the energy that can be directed toward your true desire. Especially in Satsang, when you are confronted with this desire and when this desire becomes more conscious, its counterpart doesn't sleep either. It is necessary to be absolutely vigilant because in some way the desire not to be free will appear and also wants to make itself heard. You just have to wait for it. Suddenly it will break through. The whole of humanity is ruled by the desire not to be free. This is a mystery.

* * *

The landing or bleeding off of the one true desire into other desires is a recurrent problem, because as soon as you are not in contact with your true desire, there is no chance of it being fulfilled. There are very few people in total contact with the desire to give up suffering. It is very rare to come across anyone like that. Almost everyone clings to unfulfilled desires including spiritual seekers and people who take themselves for such. Perhaps they *also* have the desire to give up suffering, but in the desire for true freedom, no other unfulfilled desire can be there. This desire is either there *exclusively* or not at all. When I say exclusively, I am not saying ninety-nine percent; I am saying one hundred percent. One hundred percent means you are ready to meet this desire for freedom unconditionally! If this desire is not met unconditionally, it's not a problem for anyone, but I guarantee you that this desire will not be fulfilled. The moment you don't give this desire one hundred percent but give it only ninety-nine percent, mysteriously, only one percent is fulfilled.

It is a real mystery why no one gives this desire a hundred percent. Perhaps there are some people who flirt a little with the desire for self-liberation, who toy with it a little and consider it intellectually. Then there are seekers who touch this desire but return once again to other desires. The temptation of what the other desires apparently have to offer is too big. And there can be experienced, of course, the deception that the desires are fulfilled. But true fulfillment never happens. You can count yourself lucky when this true desire is available to you and you are aware that it's deeper than any other desire.

Why don't I want to see this one desire?

Because you still hope and wait for the fulfillment of the other desires. The hope for fulfillment in the future is part of the mechanism of an unfulfilled desire. This one desire I speak of is not a desire that will be fulfilled in the future, it is a desire that is fulfilled *now!* Every other desire will apparently be fulfilled in the future. But when is the future?

To me it often sounds as if you are saying that I refuse.

That's right, I am saying that you refuse. It sounds absurd and possibly incomprehensible for the mind, but what I am speaking about is totally available to you in this moment, is it not? Aren't there now, as ever, tendencies in you that for many different reasons are not completely interested in freedom?

It is true that you are sitting here to get to the point of giving everything? Are you willing to give up all other desires attached to the world, attached to yourself, attached to some thing, or attached to some person? Nothing can be said about when you will get to this point of readiness. Maybe now is the time.

Naturally, the mind will say, "But I have given up so much already." I am not talking about giving up "much." The mind, by its nature, lives from deficiency and everyone identified with the mind in some way lives from deficiency too. It is not possible to counterbalance or transform this deficiency. There is only the possibility of getting to the point of being ready to give up every desire you cling to. And this is not a process. It is one moment. It is the moment of spiritual maturity, the moment you are fed up with the beggar's existence, the struggle for survival, the futile fight for recognition, the fight for power, for superiority, or whatever promises of fulfillment the mind leads you to believe. And it is exactly this moment that you will keep finding in the lives of those who have attained to this natural state of inner bliss. As Poonjaji once said, "It takes a prince to wake up."

Isn't the desire for freedom just one last concept created by the mind?

This is true. But as long as you have the belief that the concept of liberation leads you toward liberation, then use this concept. Ramana compares it to a stick by which a fire is kindled but which ultimately burns away in the fire too. The choice is made and then the choice itself will also burn away. The desire for freedom is also a concept, but perhaps it is the only useful concept.

* * *

You often tell us to let burn away in consciousness all the concepts and emotions that create suffering. But how do I start this fire?

When I say it is possible to let everything that appears in consciousness burn away without touching it, I am not speaking of a technique that the mind can learn. The *thinking mind*, especially one on the spiritual path, most often employs this strategy: "What do I do to destroy myself, to snuff out my existence? Let's see, first, I will meditate. Then I will learn many kinds of different techniques to reform and purify myself. Then I will cleanse the body and do workshops for clearing my feelings, and then I will be ready."

Ramana told a joke that applies to this, a joke about a robber who disguised himself as a policeman and pursued himself.

Everything I say could be misunderstood as a technique. No particular technique can cause tendencies of the mind to burn completely away in consciousness and not create karma. Burning *happens* on its own. Tue longing is the fire, and this fire burns away everything. It burns away your entire, never real, personal story. It burns away all of your feelings, concepts, and images.

True longing is the impulse of the search for truth. If you do not interfere, there is enough nourishment for the flame of longing to burn on its own. This flame is like a vortex that pulls you deeper and deeper. Your tendency is to hold on somewhere, to avoid this vortex and get sidetracked by thoughts, automatic patterns, habits, and emotions. For this reason the movement into the depths of yourself gets postponed, and the burning of pure longing is interrupted again and again.

The difficulty seems to be lighting the fire in the first place, to light this flame and no others, for the mind keeps other fires burning as well, other longings, desires, and interests. But these fires are not the burning of which I speak.

The other flames that burn are what is called karma. Karma is the eternal cycle of false longings and desires to which the mind has surrendered, which then have consequences, and which, most importantly, are never fulfilled. Whenever one longing is not fulfilled, the mind skips over to the next level, and there begins the endless spiral of longings that are never fulfilled. Even though they are never fulfilled, each time they are not, a little amount of credibility remains that rekindles your hope that they will still be fulfilled. This little spark of hope keeps all the other flames burning and keeps you from lighting this one flame that is the conscious impulse to search for final self-liberation. And even then, all kinds of strategies still try to keep this flame from penetrating to the depths like a vacuum that burns everything away. Yet, once this flame has been lit, ultimately nothing can extinguish the fire, for then it actually burns on its own.

You say it is the flame that keeps the search for self-liberation alive. But isn't it enough to recognize that there is no search and that there is simply the flame?

I didn't say that the flame maintains the search for self-liberation. I said that the initial moment this flame is lit is the moment that the search begins, and from this moment on, everything happens on its own. The flame is the process of burning away. This process of burning away is not what the mind comprehends as the search. Burning away has nothing to do with searching.

Paradoxically this burning away happens without anyone being there who has to search. There is no predicting how long this burning away will last, how intense it will be, or when it will be finished.

Dying into the Unknown

It is all about something to which you have been completely blind, something invisible, something that words can only point to, something that cannot be understood, something so close to you, you simply cannot see it because it is what you *are*.

Your attention is always directed toward some object. This is your habit, and the habit of every human being. It is only by directing the attention toward an object that the "world" first comes into being. At this moment of directing attention toward an object, you are blind to the one who thinks, blind to the one who feels, blind to the one who gives life to all these objects. To leave every object behind requires complete readiness and maturity. This is the readiness to die.

Thoughts are equally objects, and objects offer an illusion of the possibility of escaping death. For this reason, there is a continuous clinging to any kind of object. It does not matter whether these objects are on the apparent outside or the apparent inside.

What are you ready to give up? What are you ready to leave behind?

Any attachment to the transient body or to thoughts and feelings undoubtedly leads to some kind of Self-deception. People live for what is transient, and the mind pretends that death is far away. But death is tangibly close. Surrender is all about the readiness to die *now*.

The mind also fools you by making you believe in a very credible way that the death of the body is something terrible. I once read the report of a man who went down on a shipwrecked ferry with 900 people aboard in the winter of 1996. He described the moment he found himself in the cold water, the incredible panic and terror, and the enormous self-contraction in the face of death. He did not die, of course, otherwise he could not have written the report. But what was interesting was what happened the moment he was able to let go of this agony. It was the moment in which this man, who probably had no previous spiritual experiences nor had ever been on the spiritual search, experienced bliss. This bliss totally transcended the pain of the cold water and everything else, and it happened the moment he was ready to die.

This is the great paradox. Life, real life, can only be experienced out of a readiness to die. Real life is exactly what the mind is searching for by cutting out death in all of its subtle or gross ways. But dying actually happens in every moment, not just the moment the body dies.

I remember when I asked myself for the first time, What am I ready to let die? It didn't even start with the body. It began with the car, the most trifling of matters. It seems absurd, but in a way, it seemed worse to me if certain belongings died rather than if the body died.

It takes constant strain, constant tension, to hold your own against an inevitable death. Total readiness to die, however, is the gateway to bliss. If this body has to be taken, if it has to be sacrificed, it has to be sacrificed. Exactly the same way many living beings are sacrificed every day so that our own organisms can survive. Death is part of a totally natural process.

The Not-Self is what needs to be radically rejected. This is what I mean by the readiness to die. It is the moment in which out of total readiness for Self-recognition, the body is rejected, feelings are rejected, senses are rejected, and thoughts are rejected in order to see what remains. What remains is *Reality*. But that can neither be believed nor understood. It can only be *directly* experienced. As long as there is not a total readiness to die, there will always be something that makes you cling to the world. That does not matter. Almost everyone plays this game.

Asceticism really has nothing to do with it. I don't talk about living in an ascetic way. When I say reject, I do not mean to take any action. Rejecting means to take back the attention. Rejecting, in the spiritual sense, is no action at all.

* * *

Can you say something about being uncompromising?

Uncompromising is the force of *Shiva.** It is the readiness for destruction, which is what I call, in a slightly provoking manner, "the spiritual readiness for violence." It is the readiness to experience this core of violence that has taken so many perverted forms, and the readiness to recognize it as the force of Shiva destroying ignorance and cutting through it with its sword.

I still remember the exact moment when I experienced the force that was attached to fear and all sorts of concepts about social and personal existence. In the moment an unwillingness to compromise appeared, the fear suddenly withdrew into the background.

I wrote to Gangaji: *"The time of compromising is over!"*

This is the moment when you are really ready to be alone. This being alone is beyond apparent relationship, for any relationship with an object is ultimately an avoidance of being alone. And I know you understand what I mean. Many will misunderstand and think they have to give up their relationships. But that is not what I am saying.

Other people are not what they seem to be and neither are you. Relationship is nothing but a relationship between one illusion and another illusion. No relationship exists between you and another person. *You* are completely without relationship.

The unwillingness to compromise is what I also quite often call ruthlessness. Ruthlessness is the force that cuts your relationship with illusion, your relationship with images, masks and roles. And that includes the readiness to give up the wish to please, the readiness to go up against the status quo, for this will not necessarily be appreciated by the mind, and other people identify with this mind. When this force of Shiva appears and is in truth, resistance can be created and dust gets kicked up.

In this "unrelatedness," you will naturally search for contact with people through whom the *Self* shines. Self to Self is the only existing relationship. All dualistic relationships are empty concepts. Concepts of mother, father, child, family, friend, girlfriend, fiancé, partner, and so on, are concepts of the mind. Stay with this unwillingness to compromise, for the unwillingness to compromise is the readiness to give everything, to leave everything behind. Then you step out of this narrow prison of the mind called, "Me and my relationship. Me and my little world." You open to the splendor of the Self with no relationship and no clinging.

Teacher and Student in the Teaching of Non-Teaching

How do you define a spiritual teacher? Is there a difference between a teacher and a master?

This is merely a question of terminology. I lean towards the terminology Poonjaji used, which is that of teacher and priest. According to that terminology, a true teacher essentially has nothing to teach. Teachers who declare themselves true teachers but who teach concepts, Poonjaji called preachers.

There are many teachers, I would say almost all, who teach on diverse levels of understanding and, as long as they "teach," I would also call them preachers. They can be teachers that teach in different traditions, they can be teachers that don't teach traditionally, they can be therapists; it doesn't matter. There is no general rule about it. By some very good luck, I personally happened to meet a teacher through whom the final knowing was transmitted. Teachers through whom the final knowing is transmitted are as rare as a needle in a haystack. It doesn't matter whether a teacher claims to be enlightened or not. People who claim to be enlightened are not enlightened anyway, and people who don't claim to be enlightened, aren't either.

A preacher teaches concepts; a true teacher *empties* concepts.

A teacher whose teaching is beyond concepts can, of course, teach within concepts temporarily in order to deal with the student's limited level of understanding. *Temporarily.* The teacher always works with the student on the student's level of understanding. Concepts can be useful to temporarily satisfy the *thinking mind* and then lead it to the next higher level. Don't imagine however, that any level of concept is the ultimate level of knowing.

So, only somebody who has realized the ultimate truth can distinguish a preacher from a true teacher?

For the *thinking mind*, there is no ultimate possibility of distinguishing because the *thinking mind* can only see, think, and understand within its own system, its own framework of understanding. Anyway, the question of how to distinguish a true teacher from a false teacher is a question of the *thinking mind* and therefore theoretical.

When an authentic longing reaches the degree where it exceeds other longings and desires, this authentic longing will find its way to a teacher. So-called false teachers, or preachers, fulfill a perfect purpose at a limited level of recognition, an understanding that still mostly occurs on a reflective level within the structures of the *thinking mind*.

Can you describe what such a reflection looks like from your own life, for instance with earlier teachers?

Earlier in my life, I was not seeking freedom. I was seeking some distorted kind of power or magic, and this search manifested a teacher who worked equally with these powers. A teacher who, through his own false understanding, identified with powers, and who worked a lot with the misuse of power. Use and misuse are ultimately the same. I could go so far as to say that in reality there is no misuse of power, but in any case, it became very clear that this teacher was a reflection of the shadow of my own mind, mirrored by this relationship, and in that recognition was the possibility of going deeper.

Everybody finds the perfect teacher because what appears as the teacher is nothing but a reflection of the seeker's level of understanding. It is a natural law that for each *thinking mind, the teacher* manifests in a form that in that moment is adequate and necessary to reach a certain level of understanding. If one looks at it this way, then it's obvious that the whole question is theoretical and the search for the ideal teacher, the true teacher, is unnecessary. It is not possible to find *the teacher* by means of the *thinking mind,* but naturally and perfectly, the seeker always finds the teacher who is teaching on a level that in that moment is accessible to the student's mind and corresponds to their prevailing level of purity. Or to put it another way, a level that corresponds to the seeker's level of arrogance.

All preachers are only reflections of the One Teacher. Those reflections are simply distortions originating from the interventions of a seemingly individual mind, the illusory reality of which has not yet been extinguished. Whenever this is the case, the pure teaching of non-teaching is distorted and falsified by certain hidden motivations and becomes a "teaching." This distortion can become very subtle, as can be seen, for example, through the Enneagram.

For me, one of the essential recognitions about ego-structure is that the ego, through Self-denial or Self-obliviousness, can ascend to high pseudo-spiritual levels. And, as can be easily imagined, this ego can of course appear even as a saint who apparently acts out of selfless love and who makes no personal demands, etc. But in understanding that the ego can function in almost total Self-obliviousness, that on a very deep level anger or suppressed instincts can still be hidden, then it is possible to see that the ego is still functioning on an unconscious, pre-rational level. It is a kind of fusion, a kind of unrealized awareness of oneness that has not passed through certain phases of separation and individuation.

As soon as there is any kind of identification, no matter how high the levels on which it is occurring, including that of the spiritual teacher, then immediately, suffering occurs. Suffering has to immediately arise because dissociation happens, because "you" and "I" come into being. The "I" that *always* takes itself for something special comes into being, and in this case it is saying, "Now I am the teacher, and therefore I am something special."

Suffering also occurs whenever there is identification with the role of the student. Now it is the suffering of, "I do not have what the teacher has."

Identities are naturally very attractive, especially when the roles being played involve power, prestige, or importance. There are infinite possibilities of identities and roles, all of which are voluntarily adopted.

A teacher will always only teach whatever corresponds to his own limited understanding. It is not possible, even conceptually, to go deeper than one's own understanding. And as long as there is structure or conditioning, in the sense of a *thinking mind*, this conditioning will develop a teaching that can only approach *Reality*.

*   *   *

On the relative level of the closed system of the *thinking mind*, there are people who have reached advanced levels but cling to them forever, causing their development to stop. My experience is that people have simply reached advanced levels of understanding but have not left the closed system of the intellectual mind, and that in itself becomes a hardening and a trap. Then there is no longer any openness for discrimination and, on a very advanced level, it is precisely this discriminating power of the intellect that gets undermined.

This trap of the mind is especially dangerous when the mind is in the role of the teacher or therapist without being in direct contact with a realized guru. Then the ego can express itself through conceptual knowledge and scholarship, and hence through levels that most seekers can no longer differentiate between conceptual knowledge and truth because the levels are so subtle. Only people who have reached or exceeded a similar level can perceive the difference.

In the reality of No-Mind, all of these so-called levels do not exist. They only exist within the closed soap bubble of the *thinking mind*. Anyone who really *believes* in the reality of these levels has not left the constructs of the mind.

There can be a deeply touching love radiating through a teacher; however, that is not necessarily a sign of true realization. There can be a state of "unconscious enlightenment." This pre-egoic stage is also ego itself. As long as there is any identification with the *thinking mind*, there is blindness to one's own blindness, even though it may be minimal. The ego, although hidden, is still there in some form, for the *thinking mind* is characterized, first of all, by blindness.

* * *

The potential and the authority to realize Truth is within you. If you go to see a teacher and you believe that teacher to be outside of you, you will then have the tendency to transmit the authority for this potential to the teacher outside in order to postpone the realization. It is so much more comfortable to just *believe* what alleged authorities have to say. This is how groups of followers come into existence, by believing what somebody else is saying. The potential and the complete authority for Self-recognition are within you.

For many teachers whose realization of the *I Am* is not total, and in whom certain structures of the *character fixation** still work as before, the temptation of personal power becomes big because the students attribute to the teacher a specialness that supports the person in their own identification with seemingly personal power. Power is such a great temptation for the ego. Many teachers whose recognition of the Self is incomplete are still subject to the delusion that there is a relationship between the teacher and the student. Out of this delusion, they subtly communicate a wish for relationship with their students, a wish for power. The true teacher, who *is* the Self, has no wish for relationship with anything or anyone at all.

I don't want anything from you and you don't want anything from me. That is the truth. What a relief.

Would you then call yourself a teacher?

I do not identify with the role of teacher because this identification would be a limitation. Why should I identify with the role of teacher and limit this that *I am* to an image?

Krishnamurti did not really have an outer teacher, and to me he is one of the great exceptions. He disapproved of the teacher-student relationship and pointed out that an outer teacher is not necessary for realization. However, I can only confirm this theoretically. Experience does not indicate that it's not necessary to have an outer teacher. Absolutely not. Rather, experience shows that the *thinking mind* is much too weak to confront its own layers that are ultimately responsible for suffering, yet rather than appearing as suffering, they appear as arrogance.

Subtle layers of arrogance are not always obvious in how they create suffering. Arrogance also appears as contentment, self-satisfaction, enjoyment, sanctimoniousness, and even ecstasy. When the ego starts to give itself "purified" importance, this time on so-called spiritual levels, as for instance by identifying with the role of the teacher, then those levels are not necessarily confronted voluntarily. On top of that, when the mind is identified with "enlightenment" and lands in that identification, and then by motivations that originate in still unrecognized layers of the ego-structure starts to become independent of the outer teacher, then there is a relapse into suffering. There is self-inflation and spiritual megalomania in the name of "enlightenment." This has happened again and again to both teachers and students.

Poonjaji once said that ashrams never worked.

I have no ambition to found a traditional ashram because I wouldn't recommend choosing a traditional spiritual path. Rather, spiritual institutions often seem to be in danger of becoming an obstacle on the path toward liberation. This is because the mind of the seeker who then leads the institution often corrupts the enlightenment, originally alive, impersonal, and without any concepts, and changes it into a teaching of concepts. This teaching of concepts then becomes part of the institution, and in that moment, there inevitably arises an instinct for survival, which gains power in proportion to the growth of the institution.

Experience does not show that traditional ashrams release liberated people in the most direct way. Usually, these ashrams maintain illusory student-teacher relationships instead of outgrowing them. Even modern ashrams like Osho's have ultimately missed the mark. If enlightenment becomes a threat to the ashram, this is utterly absurd, such as for instance the ashram management in Poona tried to stop people from going to see Shri Poonjaji.

Does this mean that you absolutely disagree with traditional paths?

No, for some people a traditional spiritual path is totally consistent with what they need. I do not absolutely disagree with anything. How can I absolutely disagree with anything and then say there are no rules?

Favoring or disagreeing with any spiritual path very often leads to further boundaries, separations, and sectarianism, which ultimately means that the *thinking mind* identifies once again with being special. How many spiritual seekers are there who think they are special, who think they have now outgrown the ignorance of normal people? These are just deeper levels of self-deception having their origin in the arrogance of the *thinking mind.*

My recommendation is simply to lead a totally normal life and to be still. Stillness will sooner or later touch *ordinariness.*

It is essential for you to always know you are in contact with the teacher, that you are in the teacher's embrace, and that you are never left alone. If you feel left alone or lonesome, it means that you have left the teacher alone. You should never place the responsibility on the teacher for being left alone or for feeling left alone. Always take that responsibility upon yourself. In truth, you always get the support you really need, even if it does not correspond to your preconceptions. In truth, you are always totally immersed in your true wish, which is to be in peace, and this is a self-fulfilling wish.

One has only found the true teacher when the flame has been transmitted. Is that correct?

Yes, that is correct.

So, only when one has realized truth through the outer form of the teacher has the teacher really appeared?

That is correct, but even so, it is still possible that the cloud cover created by the mind's continuous agitation can be broken through without the teacher. And in that short glimpse, the inner knowing which has always been there is awakened. It's true that the inner knowing can, and most likely will, be covered again, but once the cloud of mind has been broken through, it never totally clouds over again. The sky can almost seem totally obscured, but once there has been this contact, I can say from my own direct experience that it doesn't totally cover over again. There remains this kind of access to natural being, to the Self. Then the Self begins to recognize Itself, the teacher. Naturally, this access is only complete the moment the flame is transmitted and the realization is total. Then one realizes that in reality, there is no cloud cover and there never has been.

*   *   *

What does it mean to "turn away" from the teacher as opposed to "stay with" the teacher? It can't really have anything to do with whether you are in direct contact with the form of the teacher or not, correct?

"Turning away" is an inner turning away, having nothing to do with whether there is outer contact or not. To turn away is to once again pick up a layer of the *thinking mind*, causing dissociation and an illusory boundary between you and the teacher. The moment there is a boundary between you and the outer teacher, there is also a boundary between you and "others," between you and the world, between you and your own heart. In fact, this no-boundary between you and the teacher is nothing other than *Being* with the heart.

Whenever a boundary reappears, whenever the *thinking mind* resumes control, it is reflected in everything and suffering is recreated. Possibly then, a "teaching" resumes and is passed on. Whatever is resumed, it is simply the phenomenon of the *thinking mind* functioning again as the teacher but not as the *Self*. And then if the *thinking mind*, still working as before, also becomes conscious of the limitation, this is already the deeper teaching of the true teacher. It is undeniably true that the true teacher shows through everybody. Naturally, even the "false" teacher, the imitation of the true teacher, is also ultimately in the service of the *One Teacher*.

It still needs to be understood that there are also masters or teachers who did not receive the "flame" from another teacher but realized the truth directly.

It is possible. Ramana, for instance, received the transmission from the mountain, Arunachala, but it is certainly most rare. The teacher is not confined to the human form and can also appear and teach through other forms, material as well as invisible. There is no limitation. If the teacher appears through forms that are not human, in spite of that there will always be a very special connection,

as there was between Ramana and Arunachala. It is a very
deep feeling of love that will never cease as long as the
body exists.

Self-Inquiry

Who Am I?

Self-inquiry is *one* question exclusively, and that is the question, *Who?* It is not the question, *What?* It is not the question, *Why?* It is not the question, *How?* Self-inquiry is only one essential question and that question is, *Who?.*

* * *

Self-inquiry, as Ramana taught it, and what I call the *Great Self-inquiry** has nothing to do with the self-inquiry portrayed by psychologists and esoteric teachers. That is what I call *small self-inquiry,** an inquiry into the contents of the mind. The Self-inquiry I speak of is an inquiry that without a single thought directly *sees* the origin of all thought.

* * *

Who Am I? is the only question directed toward the subject. All other questions are directed toward objects. The subject is what you seek, the seeker himself, and that is what has to be recognized. The moment you direct the search toward objects, you will only find objects, and when you find objects, you find something that is separate from you. When you find something that is separate from you, you suffer. The separation between subject and object, between I and you, between I and thoughts, between I and something else, is the human condition. But if you stay with the question, Who Am I? the question that Ramana called the only true question, you can go deeper than any object appearing in your mind.

Everything you experience is an object in your mind, and your attention is continuously directed toward these objects. At first, attention is directed toward objects on the so-called "outside," and the mind looks for fulfillment in outside objects — a partner, a child, a mother, a father, material possessions, and all kinds of things. When the mind eventually turns inward in meditation, its attention is still directed toward objects, only now they are objects on the "inside" — images, thoughts, feelings, or body sensations.

To stay with the question *Who am I?* requires not dwelling on any other questions or thoughts. *Who am I?* is neither a thought nor a mantra. It is as if you direct the question, without directing it, toward stillness itself and remain present with the question. Stay in the presence of the question. You need not continuously repeat it. If you are in the presence of the question, this question will lead you deeper and guide you to its own origin. The origin of this question is the origin of all thoughts, and this origin of thoughts is what you are searching for.

* * *

Every problem appearing in your life is ultimately insignificant. What is essential is the root of all problems, and this is actually the only problem. It is contained in a harmless letter, and this letter is *I*. Almost every thought that appears in your consciousness starts with this letter.

Investigate the reality of this I-thought. Following the I-thought back to its origin is what Ramana called Self-inquiry and what Poonjaji called the quickest way to enlightenment.

There are so many therapies and spiritual teachings, and it is surprising, isn't it, how insignificant the results actually are, how few people actually live in the continuous experience of bliss? It seems to me that any "teaching" is preoccupied with the insignificant, with changing, improving, or manipulating the contents of the mind instead of getting to the core of the suffering, which is this letter *I*. When you reach *I*, you are very close. Everything else is insignificant.

One of the few spiritual qualities of the mind is the ability to refuse the insignificant and get directly and absolutely to the essential. This radical totality refuses any spiritual concept that has ever been taught. Everything has its place. But if you are ready for Satsang, this complete realization is possible *now*, only *now*. Millions of thoughts are reduced to *one* thought, and this one thought is reduced to one letter, which is *I*. It is possible in a split second to leave behind all the millions of thoughts and to direct total attention toward *I* and the question, *Who am I?*

* * *

How do I recognize who I am?

Nobody knows, because nobody ever *really* asks this question, in this moment, regardless of the consequences. The potential for the answer to this question is already in you. It is only available at this moment and no other. The thinker has the habit, the deep conditioning or imprinting, of not being willing to receive the answer or of postponing the answer to some future time. The truth is you can absolutely receive the answer in this moment.

Mikaire, an Advaita teacher from New Zealand said, "If you were offered $60,000, you wouldn't hesitate a moment to give everything to find the answer in this moment."

But perhaps, as most people do, you need to prepare for this question by first investigating what you are not. That is what therapy is. Therapy is occupied with what you are not. Esoteric teachings are exclusively occupied with what you are not. Once you get more and more insight into what you are not, once you get insight into the transitory nature of the structures of mind, the transitory nature of *I*, you are perhaps then ready to turn to the true essential question, *Who am I?* You are no longer asking who you are not. No system or teaching deals with who you really are. You cannot deal with who you are. You can only deal with objects, not with the subject.

The only method, which is actually no method at all, is the question, *Who am I?* Stay with this question, and the moment an I-thought appears, follow this I-thought to its origin. Ramana applied this method, and it is the only method that will directly destroy the I-thought. It's simple and obvious to recognize this I-thought, which you have been occupied with your whole life as the source of suffering. Explore its origin. Not by further thoughts, but *directly*. When the thought appears, inquire into its origin by following the thought, with your attention, back to its source.

It's obvious, isn't it, that this I-thought keeps the whole structure of identification together? It keeps your whole story together. It keeps the whole world together. The I-thought is the reference point for everything. Who are you in this moment if the thought, *I*, disappears? When the I-thought appears, it seems so natural that you believe you *are* it. It seems natural because it has been taught to you since the birth of the body. No one ever taught you anything else. For this reason, you *automatically* identify with the I-thought as soon as it appears. This is not a conscious process. The thought, *I*, appears and automatically *becomes* "I."

Perhaps you are ready to experience what is here when there is no I-thought, when for a moment you touch the stillness of yourself between the I-thoughts. In order to wake up from this trance of I-thoughts, allow yourself to have the experience of being without any thought. Direct your attention towards the *gap* between two thoughts.

* * *

Self-inquiry is possible at any moment you are ready to simply look into your heart and follow whatever makes you unhappy back to its source. Be it a thought or a feeling, notice whether or not it is real. This requires the readiness to go deeper than any concept or belief, including any spiritual concept or belief. It requires looking behind thoughts, looking behind after-thoughts, looking behind everything that appears.

Normally, identification happens blindly in the midst of all possible kinds of thoughts—thoughts that evaluate, thoughts that compare, thoughts that pretend to know, thoughts that pretend not to know, thoughts that make you small, thoughts that make you big, thoughts that in some way are either occupied with you or pretend to be occupied with you. All these thoughts form an artificial world, and more or less everybody takes this artificial world to be real. But what substance does a thought have? What is the true substance of any thought? What if they were not even *your* thoughts?

It is possible to get to the essence of a thought through *direct* experience. It is not about using thought to understand other thoughts. When you sit here in Darshan trying to understand with thoughts what is being pointed to, these are all just more thoughts. What I am talking about is *the moment of stopping* every thought, of sinking deeper than any thought. I call this moment of stopping the "crack," and there can be a sensation of falling deeper. This fall follows the laws of gravity, which work in the mental world as well when there is no intervention of an I-thought.

In reality, this is your natural state opening up. It is Being, Consciousness, Bliss, without any feeling, without any sensation, without anything, just *that*. It is nothing special. Suffering is what is special. How could your natural state be something special? To reach what is called enlightenment is nothing special. It is simply your natural home, where you have always dwelt. You just believed you were somewhere else.

You have attached all kinds of superstitious concepts to enlightenment, as if enlightenment was some kind of extraordinary, intense state. Just be *here*. You need not search any more. Be here and fall into what opens up to you. Realize what happens. If sensations and emotions are stirred up, very good. They are like material thrown out of a volcano into the open sky to simply dissolve into nothing.

What is the Mind?

Can you say something about how thoughts come into existence and the functioning of the human mind?

Thoughts are your worst enemies and your best friends, for they are also indirectly transmitters of true recognition. After having asked yourself what thoughts are, how they come into existence and what their function is, you can perhaps make the crucial observation that except in thought, no separation can be seen anywhere. When we say, for instance, that someone is identifying with the body, it is not the body that says, "I am so and so." The body doesn't say anything. Without the force that animates it, the body is dead. So there has to be the thought, "I am Thomas," a thought that creates a relationship between a seeming "I" and the body.

In a moment of stillness, beyond thought, you can have the fundamental experience of no separation. Then, as soon as you open your eyes, the unconscious I-thought is triggered, but at that moment, it is not usually recognized as a thought. When you close your eyes again, this unconscious I-thought is gone, and if you will examine closely, you will see, in fact, that in the moment of no thoughts, no separation is perceptible between you and others.

The separation between you and other, or you and God, or you and anything else exists only in thought. Consequently, it is easy to see that the I-thought creates a split between an unknown I and an equally unknown you, a supposed I and a supposed you, a thought of I and a thought of you. When this thought sinks back into emptiness, there is no separation. But instead of not touching the next thought that appears and is actually not yet split, instead of letting it sink back into emptiness, the habit is to continuously pursue the thoughts and be pursued by the thoughts. When you are pursued by the I-thought, you lose the direct knowing of the origin of thought.

What is the root of thought? Where is the root? What is your direct experience of a thought in the moment it appears? The I-thought is only assumed to be real, but upon investigation, it can be recognized not to be the actual experience of your *Being*.

Direct your attention now toward where the I-thought originates. What is your experience?

I see there is no root at all. And now, something is appearing from a very profound depth.

What is it?

Yes, what is it? What I see is that when I say "I," there is a falling into the split of separation.

No. The fact of saying "I" is not the entry into the split. Stay with the question, "What is the root of a thought," without getting involved in its contents and without going into analysis. What do you mean when you say, "There is no root at all"? Stay there. Stay with your direct experience.

The perception is that "I" somehow comes to the surface.

Direct your attention toward where the *I* comes from, letting it sink back in. Then you will see simply, directly, without thought.

It comes from nowhere.

Yes. Where is the assumed root of thoughts? You must have assigned some root to thoughts to be able to give them reality.

It seems to me like a accumulation? happens in a very subtle way.

What, exactly, seems like an accumulation?

An I appears, and then there is something like a chain with more and more links attaching to it.

What happened in the moment the first thought of *I* appeared?

For instance, the thought arose, "I want to know it." Then the thought suddenly gets "thick."

The subtle mistake is still in your directing attention toward the thought itself instead of the root, and that, exactly, is how it gets "thick."

Yes, it somehow gets inflated.

What happens when you follow the thought back to its origin without directing the attention toward the thought itself, as normally is your habit? What happens when you ask the question, "What is the root?"

Then there is a kind of not knowing.

Good. This is very valuable. Is "not knowing" a thought?

No.

Dive into this not knowing and examine it simply and directly without any belief or disbelief.

The thought doesn't exist.

Are you saying there is no root to the thought?

There is no root.

Yes! Thoughts do not have roots! That isn't comprehensible to the mind. If you are ready to dive totally into this recognition of the origin of thoughts, to let yourself fall into it, this is *Self-inquiry*. In this moment, the root that never existed is taken away from thought. The I-thought has no root.

Most people want to get some advice on the spiritual path — rules, teachings, what is right, what is wrong. They want to have experiences of truth and understand intellectually, but few are ready to go deeper than thought, deeper than feelings, into total meditation. This is the key.

Will there then no longer be any experiences of truth?

Yes, there are experiences, but there is no longer anyone who experiences. The separation between the experiencer and the experienced only exists in thought. When the thought disappears, how can there be anyone who experiences?

What is passed on directly through Ramana's lineage is the possibility of exploring the origin of thought, particularly the I-thought. This can only be explored *now*.

When I ask a scholar, "Who is the psyche?" the answer will necessarily come from every other moment but *now*. In other words, the psyche itself will answer. Self-inquiry, however, occurs in this moment *now*. It does not come from the psyche, from the mind, but directly from the *Self*, out of emptiness. Poonjaji said it requires courage to embrace this emptiness, for it is this emptiness that the mind is most afraid of.

Why is the mind most afraid of emptiness?

Because you believe that by diving into this emptiness, you will dissolve.

Do I?
       The *Self* remains.

* * *

Is it possible that thinking prevents the Self from becoming active?

By tensely clinging to the thinking process you prevent the realization of what you already are. Identified thinking is an incredible limitation and an imitation of true Self. The world of ideas is an artificial world, in which people live and take it for reality. Emotions belong to this artificial world as well. For thinking is not limited to the head, as many people believe. Thinking includes the emotions and even the instincts.

Do you appreciate the stillness that opens up between two thoughts? More and more a natural attraction towards the gaps between the thoughts will happen on its own, without your influence. All that is naturally required is your willingness to turn inward, your readiness for contemplation and meditation.

From I to i: The Illusory Self-Shrinking Process Through Identification with Thinking

When I ask myself the question, "Who is seeing?" what seems to appear automatically is the answer, "I." Is that all right, and should I go on asking who this "I" is after all?

Yes, it is natural that the answer "I" appears. Naturally, it is this *I* that sees, feels, thinks, acts, and so on. Yet the answer is unsatisfactory because in the next moment this *I* will already be pretending to be "somebody," to be an individual who acts, thinks, and feels. In other words, to be an *I* that is separate. When you say, "I," or "I am," this does not in itself indicate separation. However, as soon as you say, "I am so and so," or "I can, I want, I have, I should be able to," etc., as soon as you add self-concepts, separation occurs. This means that the *I* responsible for separation cannot be the same *I* that arises in the answer, "I."

But the question was, "Who sees?" and the answer is "I see." Does the separation happen when a verb is attached?

"I see" is not necessarily the separation. As long as the *I* who is seeing is not separate from what is seen or separate from the act of seeing, as long as this trinity is one, then " I see" is just the quality of the moment. When in deep sleep the "see" is dropped, still the "I" remains as the substratum for every state.

I have an intuitive knowing that I existed in deep sleep.

Yes! If you were not aware of being there in deep sleep, you couldn't upon waking in the morning say that you slept particularly well, that you enjoyed a particularly relaxing sleep. Consciousness is uninterrupted. I can say from my experience that the same is true in a near-death experience. There is a trace of remembrance of existing even after clinical death, although in this sense, there is no object to be remembered. Normally, we think of remembrance as a thinking process, whether the thinking is visual or mental.

Or remembering a dream?

Yes, that would be visual thinking. In any case, it is a dualistic experience in which there was a someone experiencing something. There was a subject and an object. A non-dualistic remembrance does not seem graspable by the human mind. It could be that deep sleep leaves something like a non-dualistic remembrance—"I" in the state of "pure consciousness" is aware of itself and experiences a trace of remembrance—but it is so elusive that it can't really be grasped by any kind of thinking.

It's like a feeling of presence.

Feeling perhaps gets closer than the notion of thought, but that doesn't really hit it either. It is difficult to use the notion of "remembrance," because normally, of course, this relates to the past, to the dimension of time. The remembrance I'm talking about is the remembrance of timeless deep sleep, and through my own subjective experience, the no-time of clinical death. It is out of time, in as much as it doesn't relate back to anything. My experience is that this remembrance of no-time is nothing but the experience of this moment *now*.

Ramana Maharshi also said that the true Self that exists in deep sleep is here now as well, and that self-realization is all about becoming aware of this state of deep sleep during the waking state. Are you also saying that the state of deep sleep is present now?

Not the state of deep sleep but the *consciousness* out of which this state is created is present now. In absolute consciousness, it is not possible to identify with anything. Yet, in spite of that, it's surprising how fast and subtly identification happens. I have found that there are layers of thought more subtle than the thoughts themselves. I call these layers "imprints" of thoughts. Imprints of thoughts have the nature of identifying with the thought in the next moment after it arises. Maybe thousands of times this same thought has arisen and you have gone into relationship with it. When there is no longer identification with an *I*, there stills remains a tendency toward movement in that direction. This is like the withdrawal symptoms from having taken a drug for thousands of years.

* * *

The crucial thing is to realize what the attention is attached to. For it is by the attention clinging to something that this process happens we call "falling asleep."

First of all, most people do not pursue awakening to the truth of who they are because they continuously cling to everything and therefore have no experience of not clinging. If a man is continuously bathing in the bathtub, and I propose to him not to touch the water, he will not understand. If you want to know how falling asleep happens, realize what phenomena you habitually cling to, whether they are thoughts, feelings, body sensations, images, or other objects. Whatever the attention is occupied with, this is exactly what keeps you from being aware, alert, and still. Clinging to something always signifies ignoring the *Now*.

Mostly we are attached to some image from the past, even if it is just from the last moment. Whenever that happens, the relationship with the Self, which *is* totally alive in this moment, cannot be recognized. You have an idea that something should be different, or something should be here that is not here, and this idea covers what *is*.

When I sat in Satsang with Gangaji, she often talked about non-identification. I really didn't understand what she meant. I thought she was talking about some kind of technique I could use in order not to identify. But there is no technique whatever that could be used in order not to identify oneself.

To be more precise, there *are* techniques to help keep from identifying, but they are only of transient value and ultimately don't lead to complete non-identification. In other words, don't try not to identify. Forget the whole thing about identification. One way of looking at it that might make it easier for you and might feel more appropriate in this moment is this: Don't take anything personally. You believe everything must have something to do with you, not necessarily because you want to feel better by it, but because you want to feel worse by it. Don't take anything personally. It has nothing to do with you. Examine just how often you take something personally and then suffer from the significance you give things that may not have anything to do with you. Nothing has anything to do with you.

Beyond the Subject/Object Relationship: The Eye Cannot See Itself

I still don't understand exactly how observing the I-thought works, how to go to the bottom of this one last thought and the essential question, Who am I?

Who says that it is about observing the I-thought?

That's what I have understood it to be.

It's not about observing the I-thought; it's about observing the one that clings to the thought.

And it doesn't matter what thought it is?

Every thought is an I-thought.

Isn't there one last or first thought, and once one has seen how it arises, liberation is here?

The truth is that every thought is the first thought and the last.

The I-thought itself has no form that is somehow extraordinary? Is it a totally normal thought, and one just has to see how it arises?

Every thought can be followed back to its root. When you speak of the first thought to which everything can be followed back, you speak from the conceptual framework of time, as if the thoughts have arisen in the evolution of time. It is possible, however, to follow a thought back *in this moment*. In this moment, there is only *one* thought.

The problem is that instead of really following the thought all the way back to its source, expression is given to further thoughts, which equally arise from deeper layers underneath the thought. To follow one single thought that arises back to its origin seems to be difficult. This is because there is a tendency to "land," and this "landing" happens by clinging to other thoughts that may also arise.

When I become more and more silent, especially in Darshan, there is a moment in which I'm waiting for the next thought to arise, and just by that waiting for a thought to arise, no thought arises.

This is the cat waiting in front of the mouse hole that Gangaji talks about. When the cat is vigilant, no mouse shows up.

You say it is not about observing the thought but about observing the observer. Can you explain that again in more detail?

Following a thought back necessarily leads to the root of the thought and thus to witnessing.

Normally, attention is split off to an object and then directed obsessively toward that object. The thought itself is also an object of perception. So there is a split between somebody who observes an object and the object observed. Obviously, just observing the thoughts is not enough to remove this split. Meditators often draw back the attention from the outside world and observe the thoughts in the inner world but remain attached to this split between themselves as observers and the thoughts that arise.

I was once caught in this prison myself. I saw every thought arise in total clarity and awareness, and yet, in a certain way, I still saw myself as a helpless observer separate from the thoughts that arose. As just another form of captivity, I was simply observing thoughts in a dissociated way, and dissociation did not remove identification. Just the opposite, it fixated the identification.

The I-thought is not aware of having an origin because every I-thought takes itself for the origin. It takes itself for the subject, and it is not aware of also being just an object. The I-thought is not aware that deeper than itself is its own creator, the true subject, impersonal consciousness itself. When this I-thought touches the stillness of consciousness, and the illusory split between the I-thought and consciousness is removed, realization occurs.

Isn't this I-thought what I understand to be "myself"?

Yes, that is exactly what I just said. On a level that is intellectually incomprehensible, you understand yourself to be the I-thought. Every I-thought understands itself to be the subject.

Consequently, I see myself as just a succession of these I-thoughts believing they are complete in themselves?

That is correct.

So, the identity I claim as "myself" is totally fake?

This identity is nothing but a succession of I-thoughts, taking themselves for the subject. It is, in truth, just one single thought, and this thought can trail a string of apparently similar thoughts something like the faint imprints of a stamp called "time" or "remembrance." But in truth, it is just one single thought arising in this moment, trailing along a string of time, and with this thought, you are identified.

Why does this thought arise?

The question "why" as I've already stated, is a useless question because it is asking for an ultimate origin. Underneath every string of "why" questions is the search for the origin itself. In asking "why" the *thinking mind* gets to the point where the question is no longer possible. This question is nothing but the entry into an endless loop of the *thinking mind* that can never be answered by itself. But to give a relative answer, the I-thought arises so that recognition can happen.

So that it can ultimately be seen through?

It is the same as the story of Adam and Eve. Adam has eaten from the "Tree of Recognition." The moment he ate from the Tree of Recognition, he fell out of paradise. Original sin and the possibility of recognition are the same.

Does that signify that eating the apple from the Tree of Recognition was the first I-thought?

Yes. The moment Adam bit into the apple, the first I-thought arose.

I experience consciousness as a kind of "black night sky," a nothing that is at the same time something, and in which I even feel good, yet I still have the feeling of being separate. I am still the one who observes this dark, black nothing. I am the observer, and nothing is the observed. Do I simply need to turn around somehow, and if yes, how can I do that?

I can't tell you any trick, any technique, any method for how to turn around. In fact, this turning around happens totally by itself out of the readiness to give up everything in that moment in which the observer sees himself. For what causes the separation between subject and object, one could say, is just the lack of readiness on the part of the illusory subject, the I-thought, to let go of whatever object it sees. The object is not attached to the subject, but the (pseudo-) subject is attached to the object.

When you are ready to give up any object for what you really are, no matter how precious it appears to you, just as you are ready every night to give up any object for the bliss of deep sleep, this turning around happens totally on its own. It happens by an act of grace, in a vacuum of longing. It happens on its own! There is nothing anyone can do for it. The only thing you could do for it, although this word "do" will most likely be misunderstood, is just to check again and again if there is the readiness to really and truly give everything. "Everything" means every object of your perception that you cling to. This relates to both objects on the outside and objects on the inside. It relates to other people. It relates to the whole world.

Usually, there is a landing on certain layers of phenomena. There may be a readiness to let go of certain objects, but the *thinking mind* selects and keeps hidden preferences. In the background, there are still certain ideas about life, certain ideas about oneself that do not even concretely appear as thoughts because they are hidden identifications that one doesn't really want to give up. At a certain level of maturity in the spiritual search, once you see these thoughts totally, nakedly, and clearly, you can no longer pretend that they express truth. If you cling to certain ideas about yourself with which you are identified, if you cling to certain contents of I-thoughts and are not totally ready to give up this attachment, these thoughts will hide in consciousness. They will withdraw from the clear view of consciousness and dive down into the subconscious. You will pretend to turn away and direct the attention toward other, mostly outside, phenomena.

We started from the question of what could help you direct the attention back to the one who sees. I answered that this could be your complete readiness, but your readiness is still distorted, restricted, or ultimately blocked by your desires and attachments. The recurring attachment to objects can also be connected to an unwillingness to look at the attachment *closely*. Thus, further distortions and separations occur.

The first split might occur when you see something, look at it, and get attached to it. The moment of attachment is when you see an "it." The primary split occurs in the moment you are no longer purely looking but rather looking at an "it." Then further splits happen because you are not ready to look *directly* at what you see. You are still looking from the corner of your eye. The corner of your eye is the subconscious. When you have reached a certain degree of maturity in the spiritual search, then what is directly looked at can no longer simply be taken as reality. It will appear as a lie, and even then, there are still subtle mechanisms of the *thinking mind*. To avoid the complete recognition of this lie, thoughts are packed and hidden into niches of consciousness.

Perhaps it depends on the definition of the word "objects." I mean, I've never seen anything but objects.

You *can't* see anything but objects, as long as you are looking at them rather than truly *seeing*. The trinity of seeing consists of the object, the subject, and the process of seeing. When you see objects, you perceive these objects to be outside yourself — the carpet, the microphone, me, and so on. Those are objects, but what is the subject?

Probably, the observer.

Who is the observer?

Me.

Who is this me?

Me.

You are too lazy to really ask yourself this question. If me were me, if it were that simple, why would you have a problem with objects? You haven't recognized who sees because your attention is continuously directed toward objects and this is the "sleep."

Why is the attention directed toward objects? Your attention is directed at objects because you want something from them, because the objects promise security or even peace, happiness, freedom, everything you search for. The objects have to promise the ultimate fulfillment; otherwise, there wouldn't be billions of people running after these promises now as before. So, I have to ask you, what do you want from the objects?

I didn't say that I wanted anything from the objects.

You didn't say that, but *I* said it.

My question is: How can there be an I when no objects are seen?

This question is answered by itself when you have settled the question of what you want from the objects. You don't see objects just like that. You see them because you want something from them.

How do I know that there is an object there?

You know that there is an object by experiencing separation. Whenever you experience separation, there is an object. Whenever there is an object, there is also a subject and a separation between subject and object. Separation between subject and object is your daily state. The separation between I and you. *You* is the object, and you want something from the you. You can only want something from the *you* when you haven't realized who *I* is.

Isn't it an absurd spectacle that an *I* that doesn't know itself searches for a *you* that it doesn't really know either. So, actually, nobody knows anybody, yet one still searches. Everyone searches. I am repeatedly surprised and at the same time fascinated with how the "I" introduces the "you," how you make statements about the "you" as if it were self-evident.

Deep down at the core, the "I" naturally knows it doesn't know anything. And to hide this fact, it gives itself the air of knowing something and then tries to transfer this "I know" to the *you* in order to prove to itself that it does know something.

Allowing the recognition of not knowing anything can be a moment of seemingly unbearable tension, for it thrusts you into your fears of annihilation. It takes the *I* into the fear of its own destruction. Not knowing is the moment of annihilation, and this is the moment of bliss. This total not knowing is the moment of innocence, the moment of experiencing Satsang with yourself. For in assigning yourself an air of knowing, this pretending "I know" is the process by which you perpetuate feelings of guilt. You think, "I know something about myself, and consequently I know something about you," and in the end you think you know something about *Being*, about Life.

In a certain way, not knowing resembles the natural innocence of a child. Although the difference between you and the child is that the child doesn't know it doesn't know, whereas you, as a mature mind in total consciousness, are capable of knowing that you don't know. And this complete understanding of "I know that I don't know" is the beginning of realization. In true not knowing, it is possible to meet everything and everyone in openness.

Openness has no special form. Openness means that anything is possible. The total oneness of Being lives out of the infinite variety of its possibilities. There is no longer any limitation on your behavior — how you have to be, how it has to be, how you don't have to be, how it doesn't have to be. And there is no limitation to your feelings — what you are allowed to feel, and what you are not allowed to feel. Anyway, the beliefs, "I am allowed," "I should," or "I must," are all the result of, "I know something." "I know, how it has to be."

Now, I want to ask you, what do you *really* know about an object?

Nothing.

Very good! If you don't know anything about the object, the question arises, what do you know about the subject?

I don't know anything about the subject either.

Wonderful. That is a very good place from which to begin Self-inquiry.

I don't understand. How can I do Self-inquiry if I don't know anything? If I don't really know anything, then there really is nothing.

This is exactly the crucial point. You have reached the place at which Self-inquiry begins. And I want to make a distinction here between Self-inquiry and the exploration of *I*.

What is usually described as Self-inquiry is, in actuality, only an exploration of *I*. The exploration of *I* begins with you knowing something. Out of this, "I know," an exploration occurs, and then you know more. Thus, knowledge accumulates and seems to expand.

What is this "I know," really? This "I know" from which you explore, where does it really come from? Do you agree with me that "I know" comes entirely from the past? You have had experiences and recognitions linked together into something that you call "I know." This knowledge comes from your experiences in the world, let us say through innumerous incarnations, in the moment of birth, in this life, as a baby, as a small child, as an adolescent etc., up to this moment where you sit here in Darshan. This is the "I know."

Are you ready, once and for all, to drop this burden of "I know" even while noticing the tendency of wanting to immediately refill the hole with a new "I know"? True Self-inquiry is neither "I know" nor "I don't know." It is to drop everything.

* * *

The moment that the mind experiences the shock of not being able to overcome itself, the tendency appears again to travel down the same old trodden path of, "I am allowed, I can, I must, I shall," in order for the ego to save itself again. Give that up, too. But the attachment to and identification with thinking cannot just simply be given up. It requires a seeker ready to give *everything* for freedom.

Whoever is not ready to give everything will also never be ready to meet the annihilation approaching on the horizon when thinking relaxes. That is the moment when death enters the stage, only this death is not what you believe it to be. You have never trusted the direct and total experience of *now* by being still for even one single moment. If you are not interested in the direct and total experience of *now*, then you will stay with whatever your latent beliefs are about death. This is no problem for anyone except you. Any viewpoint you adopt, any opinion you pretend to have, is nothing but belief, and thus inessential.

How boring it is to exchange opinions based on belief when nobody really knows *who* it is that holds the opinions. First, find out who you are. Then if you hold opinions and viewpoints, no problem. But to not know who it is that holds an opinion or a viewpoint, and to blindly hold on to opinions and viewpoints and act from there, trying to bring these opinions and viewpoints into the "world," fighting against supposed "others" who hold other opinions and viewpoints, what a joke this is. What a joke!

The "world" as it appears to you is also just thoughts. Get rid of everything. Empty yourself totally. Then you are free. Then you recognize that who you are has always been free. What makes you believe you are imprisoned, what keeps you burdening, limiting, and restricting yourself is all of your objects of thinking, all of the concepts, thoughts, and beliefs that you think to be reality. Your only bondage is just this one thought, and this thought is *I*. Are you ready to let go of your identification with that thought? The knot of bondage consists of your identification with the I-thought. It is in this moment of identification that impersonal consciousness has infected itself with the I-thought.

*   *   *

Is the perception of phenomena already a limitation?

The limitation is not in the phenomena, but rather in attention being directed toward the phenomena, toward what is perceived instead of at what is perceiving. Ultimately, it doesn't matter what appears. The problem is that the one who perceives gets denied because in the moment you perceive something, you are caught in the triangle of perceiver, perceived, and perceiving. In that moment, there is an apparent separation and split, for what you perceive is perceived to be an object outside of yourself. You think of perception as occurring within yourself, but when you tell the truth, you see that it is outside of yourself.

When you merge with an object, for instance, with your lover, it is a transient experience, lasting only for a short time. The merging that you long for can never really be obtained through the physical. Merging with objects can never be obtained. The truth is, merging, as such, is a concept based on the idea that there is someone other than yourself to merge with. There is no one who merges, nothing that needs to be merged, no object and no subject, for all of those are only constructions of the I-thought.

The moment you believe, "I see something," or "I perceive something," this is thinking. It is already based on the illusion and the belief that there is a personal *I* who perceives. Do you see how deeply this belief is embedded? Who perceives? Who perceives *now?*

By perceiving a thought, it becomes something observed, and then there are restrictions again.

Where is the restriction? When you have the feeling of restriction, place your attention directly into the restriction and check and see what is separate from what Check it out. What is your experience?

My experience is that whenever I direct my attention to what is being perceived, separation occurs.

Do you see that the observer is also just a thought? That's the joke.

By all that we perceive, we automatically become observers?

Precisely, and I say, give up observing. This is the problem. How can you *be* when you are busy observing something. Whatever you observe appears to be outside of you. Observation fixates the attention on something outside yourself and takes you away from the consciousness of *yourSelf*, from Being, from Consciousness and Bliss — *Sat-Chit-Ananda*.

Observing is still an effort. Satsang means to give up any effort and enter wholly into the unknown of this moment. Satsang is to explore what *is*. Only from this attitude of No-Mind is it possible to understand, without a thought, for true understanding happens without a single thought or the least amount of effort.

* * *

What you take for perception is in reality a combination of an interpretation of the mind and the use of the senses in service to this mind that has not realized the truth of itself. To give up the mind seems rather frightening because you don't know who is at work then. But the mind feigns normality. Everything seems totally normal, just as it always has been. Only when you look for a moment very directly into the phenomenon itself, beyond the name the mind has given it, does this normality suddenly disappear, this taking for granted that things are as they are. These are adopted concepts, but not your actual experience. What if there is nobody in a body expressing itself?

This idea somehow gives me the creeps.

When the fixatedness of perception is suddenly interrupted, it can feel somewhat sinister because fixated perception goes by certain assumptions and interpretations that you take as a matter of course. When you examine these conventional beliefs for the first time in Satsang, you suddenly notice, hat it is not evident that there is a 'someone' in this body who expresses himself." Language points to that convention, language is structured in a way that makes believe there is a "someone" expressing himself. The body is given a name, an image arises, but where does this image arise from? Isn't it from time and space, but not at all from *now*? You knock on the door this instant and find there is nobody. You always started out from the premise that there is somebody, and suddenly you knock on the door and there is nobody. Fall into the emptiness and you will lose *nothing*.

*   *   *

I invite you to recognize where all form and content arises from, to recognize the source of form and content.

By source, do you mean the mind?

No. What you call "mind" is not your direct experience but rather a pretense of knowledge which is itself content. But content can't recognize its source. What is it that the eyes cannot see?

They can see everything. They can see feelings. They can also see through something.

Imagine eyes that have attained the highest possible degree of sensitivity and can penetrate anything. Profoundly, in their highest possible sensitivity depending on how they have been trained, the eyes are capable of seeing the most subtle forms. But what is it they can't see? The big trap of illusion in which the mind gets caught again and again is the illusion that you can see yourself. What eyes can't see is themselves.

But we see them when we look into the mirror.

No, you don't see the eye itself, you see the reflection of the eye, and you mistake the mirror image for the eye itself. You haven't recognized *who* sees. This question remains unanswered.

How can eyes see themselves? Eyes can only see objects. When you look into a mirror, there is only an object. The mirror has to be destroyed.

You cannot see your *Self.* If you could see your *Self,* it would be an object. And once it is an object, it is a reflection. You can only see reflections of your *Self.* This understanding is radical. The misunderstanding occurs when you take these most subtle reflections like feelings for truth and confuse them for the Self. But these are still only reflections in a shop of mirrors, and you get lost in the labyrinth of reflections until you recognize *who* it is that sees all of it. This is *you!* The source of all.

* * *

What keeps you from simply relaxing the mind? What keeps you from leaving the mind in peace? It is something much more simple than anything you could ever imagine. You need not observe anything, and you need not, not observe anything. It is not about your efforting to do something. What if you simply, just for a moment, gave up any effort to do anything. To give up effort means to give up resistance. It means to give up fear, or any doing, or any having to go somewhere else except where you already are. You can leave behind every concept of needing to observe something or not being allowed to observe something.

When you are aware of being aware, it is totally natural that everything arises. There is no longer a subconscious. It doesn't require any effort or concentration of consciousness to notice something appearing in consciousness. When the sun shines you don't need a torch. When I say that it is all about observing something, this is just a transitory aid to assist in the possibility of falling deeper. In reality, there is nothing to observe. You think you have to make an effort, but it is all about giving up precisely this effort, just for a moment.

Realization: The Fall into the Bottomless

Realization is an unfathomable phenomenon. It has no landing place. In a timeless moment, there is a falling into what has no end. It is the fall into the bottomless.

Realization is not a process. Understanding is a process, and genuine understanding follows realization. The moment of realization is like the bursting of a soap bubble. In the moment of realization, all knowing is available, and yet in that moment, there is no thought. Realization can never be attained by thoughts. Understanding happens through thoughts. Truth is revealed when all thoughts are stilled. It is the great misunderstanding of theoretical philosophy that realization is attained through any effort of thinking. Realization is a moment of no thinking. It is a moment of No-Mind.

The discrimination between understanding and realization is essential. Understanding takes place within the closed system of the mind. In the moment of realization, no mind can be found separate from consciousness. When the apparently separate individual mind touches pure consciousness, realization occurs.

Can this discrimination also be applied to everyday situations?

No. As a function of the *working mind,** understanding is responsible for everything that can be known.

Is there only one realization? Aren't there first several steps that give you a certain realization, and then another realization follows later, and so on?

Seen from an absolute point of view, there is only one realization, and that is Self-realization.

And then everything is over?

Realization happens in a timeless moment of grace. What is not over is the process of understanding.

Yes, but couldn't there be several realizations, again and again, in particular moments? One could also say several enlightenments?

Self-realization happens only once.

Are you sure about that?

Why should it happen several times?

A deepening, so to speak.

Yes, I can confirm this deepening, but I would describe this deepening as the mind's falling into realization, the *working mind's* fall into the Self. And this deepening has no end as long as the organism is maintained.

Is there a particular background to what you say?

What I am saying only points to a paradox that is my own direct experience. On the one hand, realization is the end, but on the other hand, it is also the beginning of deeper inquiry. The mind of the seeker flirts with the possibility of total realization and repeatedly makes its way to the edge of the abyss to look down for a moment. This process can also be called the process of understanding. Often one tries to understand intellectually what truth is all about in order to be able to deal with it. Do you really believe that one could calculate in advance the fall into what has no bottom? Understanding is the mind's attempt to eliminate risks and side effects in order to handle the fall.

Indeed, partial realizations sometimes arise out of understanding. However, that realization of which I speak, the realization of *yourSelf,* is not a process. It is the moment you have made your way to the abyss, to the edge of the cliff, and you are ready to fall. This readiness, this total readiness, is already the fall. This is the moment total realization happens, and it happens only once. It happens immediately, as Poonjaji said, in the twelve-millionth part of a twinkling of an eye.

It is important to distinguish between two kinds of knowing. One kind of knowing is the knowledge attained when you stand in front of something and look at it. Being in front of it means that there is a "preconception" of it, not a "conception." This kind of knowing is very limited and does not perceive the essence of what is being seen.

The second kind of knowing is *inner* knowing, the knowing received when any preconception is given up. In this "conception," *the knower,* the one who knows, the object of knowing, which in this instance is the *known,* and the *knowing* itself are one. There is no longer any difference between knower, known, and knowing. What remains is *That,* the knowing that knows completely naturally, without any separation, one hundred percent. This is total surrender to suchness.

Satsang is the end of all assumptions and all beliefs. It is the entry into pure *knowing.* Knowing is not the polar opposite of ignorance. True knowing is beyond. Even ignorance arises out of knowing. Knowing is beyond the polarity of ignorance and knowledge about the known. It is not knowledge *about* anything; it is *pure knowing.* This *pure knowing* is *love*. There is no difference between pure knowing and love.

I am well aware of the danger of "understanding," and the danger of the belief in understanding. And since this non-teaching has become public, there are new misunderstandings occurring among spiritual seekers. There were people who returned from Lucknow, India, after meeting Poonjaji and then claimed, "There is nothing to do; we are all already enlightened." But this "we" or this "I" who presumes it is enlightened only proves its unenlightenment. That is un-enlightenment itself. And whatever unenlightenment thinks will also be unenlightened. Enlightenment itself becomes a thought. Then every spiritual experience is monopolized and rationalized by thought. What you need, in fact, is the courage to reject every image and every concept in order to fall endlessly.

Again and again you have had glimpses of realization. If you don't pay close attention, it seems as if in this moment of realization there is a thought. But if you really scrutinize carefully, you'll notice that the thought was not there *in* the moment of realization. It arose directly *after* the moment of realization, as a way of translation to make it available to the mind. On a deeper level, *everything* was available in that moment of realization. In the moment of pure experience, or to put it even more accurately, the moment that truth is experienced on its own, there is no thought.

Do you know the moment in which a soap bubble bursts? It is a moment of stillness. Realization comes suddenly and unexpectedly, and you haven't done anything to make it come. But frequently it comes precisely the moment you finally give up doing anything to find clarity, the moment you finally give up all efforts and the struggle *against effort, for no effort*.

Meditation is Stillness Beyond Conditions

Are you ready to let this thought-machine calm down and enter into an extremely vigilant, and at the same time relaxed, state of being here? In this natural state of being here in which thoughts pass like clouds in the sky, are you willing to simply and consciously let go all mental tension, just for a moment? In this willingness, you will suddenly realize that you don't have to do anything. You don't have to think anything, and you don't have to understand anything. This is the moment you begin to sink deeper without your doing anything for it. You are here totally and naturally. You can enjoy the sinking and the falling. You can enjoy not having to do anything and not having to not do anything. You can just be here. And you are completely aware of everything that appears.

Direct the attention back toward what perceives, back toward what is aware of everything. Let yourself fall back into the unfathomable depths of consciousness without knowing where the journey will go. It is a process that takes place all by itself. It is like a moth drawn to the flame. The moment the moth dives into the flame, burning happens all on its own.

Recently you told me it made more sense to you if I didn't meditate for some time. But you haven't told me what I should do instead.

What I am implying by that is to check whether the practice of meditation is a justification for not meditating twenty-four hours a day. Rather, it's just fifteen minutes in the morning and fifteen minutes in the evening, and in between you allow yourself to fall asleep. The mechanics of this falling asleep can be very subtle.

You have told me that there is an obvious discrepancy between your experience during meditation and your experience afterwards. This discrepancy points to the trap of the mind's misuse of meditation and splitting it off from everyday life. Meditation is not when the mind meditates. True meditation is not confined to time and space; it has nothing to do with time and space.

* * *

For a long time, the meditation that helped me not to drift off during work consisted of observing my hands throughout day. This helped a lot until recently, and then suddenly it didn't fit any more, and I became irritated.

This meditation you are speaking of is a practice. The worth of this practice consists in concentrating on a single point rather than letting the mind leap from one place to another. Even so, in the end, you are still split. When you observe your hands or anything else, you perceive what is seemingly outside yourself. You are in duality and thus in illusion. As long as you direct your attention toward images, you will fall victim to the illusion that there is some separation between you and the image. However, when you turn your attention back onto yourself, not on the body but on what is aware in this moment, you see that, that is what talks, that is what hears, that is what sees, and that is what feels. *That* is limitless. It requires no effort to be *that*. You cannot perceive it, because all that is perceivable must by necessity appear separate from you. You can only *be* it. And you *are* it already.

* * *

The noise of the fan disturbs me. I have come here to be in silence.

Who is disturbed?

The one who wants to be in silence.

Where do you want to find this silence?

The silence is here, and it is disturbed. It is here to get support, not the opposite.

I don't believe that the silence is disturbed, and I don't believe it is the fan that disturbs you.

I cannot answer to that. I can only say that this ongoing noise disturbs the depth of my inner silence.

Perhaps you are ready to examine if what you call this "noise" is outside the silence you search for. Direct your attention inward, and check if this sound is outside of the silence. If it is, check what is there between this sound and the silence.

The sound is there and the silence is there.

Where is the silence and where is the sound?

I realize that the impact of the noise depends upon where my attention is.

So, what disturbs you is really the direction of your attention?

I wouldn't express it that way.

How would you express it?

Well, I realize anger is arising, and I remember Poonjaji said, "If loud music disturbs you, do not force yourself to endure it but change the room." I think the fan is completely useless. It is not hot in this room, and its draft is disturbing.

I knew the fan would be of some importance today. You now have the opportunity to realize that it's not the fan you fight against. Rather, it is the habit you have of always believing there is something wrong. If you give up fighting and are with what *is*, you can realize the incredible simplicity of what *is*. Why do you make the fan something outside yourself?

You are *That-Which-Is*. You can recognize this when you allow the thoughts to pass instead of clinging to the contents of the thoughts, as is your tendency. It is easy to be in stillness when external stillness supports it.

Yes, that is why I'm here. In everyday life, I often find myself in situations where external conditions don't support inner stillness, and I am here because I need support.

What supports you is recognition, the recognition that meditation or stillness does not happen in a certain place and is not limited to a certain place. You cannot confine stillness to a place. Whenever you confine stillness to a place, you become dependent on that place, and you will notice that it is subject to continuous change.

I don't speak of stillness in a certain place. I speak of *stillness*. Why do you think Poonjaji went with his students to the marketplace?

Yes, I just asked myself the same thing a moment ago. In a marketplace, there are continuously changing noises: the wind in the trees, the voices of people, the rikshas. India is terribly noisy, I know, and yet the stillness remains.

Stillness is *here*. Not in India or anyplace else. Those are all simply concepts. Stillness is wherever you are. It is not reliant on outside conditions. You cannot possess stillness by manipulating what is, by believing that certain conditions are necessary for stillness to be realized.

But there are places more conducive to stillness than others.

That is *relative* stillness. That is *limited* stillness. I speak of *Stillness*, and *Stillness* means to give up the mind's continuous fight against *what is*. This fight is absolutely absurd. It makes you experience separation from the so-called "other," from the fan, from India, from stillness. Thought is what creates this separation. What happens when you go deeper than the "weather" of your thoughts? You have an idea of how it should be or how it shouldn't be. Everybody has an idea of how it should be and how it shouldn't be. This is the arrogance of the mind. The fan has been turned on inside yourself, not outside. It is *That-Which-Is*. It is hopeless to fight against *Being*.

If I can't change things, I can't. But why create additional difficulties for myself? In this case, it would be possible to turn off the fan and put an end to the disturbance on the outside.

The mind always wants something different from *That-Which-Is*. And Satsang is the challenge to be with *what is* without knowing *what is*. If you believe you know something about *That-Which-Is*, you deceive yourself. It is only your idea. The mind consists of likes and dislikes. Where do likes and dislikes come from? Whose likes? Whose dislikes? Do you see? The problem is this tense clinging to likes and dislikes that don't arise out of this moment but rather out of the past.

The problem is in the strength of these thoughts. Sometimes my thoughts are so strong that they overshadow me.

Give me an example of a thought that is so strong it overshadows you.

For instance, pain, no matter what kind. From the draft of the fan, I get a sore throat, and I dislike the pain of it.

It is totally natural to dislike physical pain. And it is also totally natural to turn off the fan if it's possible. What I'm pointing you toward is the possibility of recognizing that if it is not the fan, it is something else. There is always something wrong. Do you understand? Other people are wrong, the conditions are wrong, thoughts are wrong, etc.
What is happening when this thought overshadows you?

At that moment, I am not able to get rid of it. I am not able to sink into stillness so deeply that the thought evaporates.

How do you know that stillness is outside of this thought? This is your assumption. Again, you create conditions for stillness to be. First it was the fan. Now it is a thought.

But in that moment when the thought arises, I don't experience stillness.

You don't experience stillness because in some way or another you fight against the thought and want something different from *what is,* which, at that moment, is this thought. If you are totally with this thought, if there is no separation between you and this thought, where is the problem?

You said, "I feel overshadowed by the thought." If you feel overshadowed, there must be an *I* and a thought that overshadows the *I.* This is based on your assumption that you are separate from this thought and able to observe this thought. You create separations again and again between yourself and reality, between yourself and something that arises. The continual tendency is to create a split, to create separation. This is called suffering. When you recognize that in reality there is no separation between you and this thought, then neither can there be any separation between stillness and this thought. This thought is stillness itself. Thoughts are not outside of stillness.

It all sounds as if meditation is unnecessary.

Stillness is not limited to fifteen minutes of meditation. It is not limited to a state in which there are no thoughts. It is not limited to a state characterized by exterior stillness, etc. If you want to find stillness, you have to find it *now.*

The mind tries to create conditions. "If only the fan gets turned off, then I will be at peace. When my mother dies, then I will finally be free. When I have found my partner, then I will finally be able to be in love." Do you understand? We could go on talking for hours about the various conditions the mind continually creates for itself.

Satsang means to go deeper than conditions. Stillness is *now.* Attend to the now by giving up being occupied with something else in thought. When you are totally and completely present, you are still. Not to be still means not to be present.

* * *

Check out what supports your vigilance. Perhaps you can't just go on with your usual habits. Vigilance is about discriminating between what really supports complete Self-respect and what doesn't support it, what supports your being in meditation and what doesn't support it. Certainly there are many things you do, think, and feel, things you give space to, that don't support you one hundred percent. The obstacle is that the *thinking mind* compromises with "somehow," "sometime," "somewhere," "so-to-speak," and "maybe."

You need one hundred percent resolve. The *thinking mind* continues to misunderstand this kind of ruthlessness. The resolve is to resolutely reject or to cut off what does not support you one hundred percent.

Perhaps there are things that support you ninety-nine percent, but that just isn't enough. It is necessary to give up everything that doesn't support you and exclusively search for what does support you, one hundred percent, in everything you do, think, and feel. This is complete, absolute Self-respect. It doesn't mean to fall into obsession, if obsession is your tendency, and this could be your misunderstanding.

History shows many examples of monks, nuns, sadhus, ascetics, and hermits who radically rejected everything on the outside, led an ascetic life or retired to ashrams, monasteries, caves, and forests. Outer renunciation, however, remains totally ineffective if it is not accompanied by inner renunciation. Then outer renunciation becomes a mere ritual. And the moment the *thinking mind* is confronted again with the original temptation, for instance a monk meeting with a woman, the same thing starts all over again because the inner tendency, which is the tendency of being attached to thinking, feeling, and experiencing, has not been rejected. There is no general rule about what has to be rejected and what hasn't.

* * *

Give up effort. Give up no-effort. That is the *kôan.** It is more simple than either effort or no-effort. Why should you have to do anything? Why should you have to try hard to become what you already *are*? Nobody ever *becomes* what they are. You *are* what you are. By continuously swinging back and forth between effort and no-effort in the quest to *become* what you *are*, you deny what you are now and always. You deny the naturalness of Being because you are attached to the differences, and differences bring about comparisons.

A Zen master once said, "The only answer to a Zen kôan is in the totality of your being." Satsang is a kôan.

The Realization of the Self: No Person Becomes "Enlightened"

Many spiritual teachings, and the whole of psychology as well, are fundamentally based on the illusion of developing yourself instead of allowing impersonal development to simply *happen*. *You* do not develop. That kind of teaching is based on the illusion that there is a "somebody" who needs to develop. There is nobody who needs to develop. Development is simply a change in the illusion, a change happening in the play. In Hinduism this is called *Leela,** the divine play. In this development, there can be no development from imperfection to perfection. Throughout any development, there is always, only perfection. Related to the personality of a human being, this means that perfection cannot be found in an imagined future ideal but rather in this very moment.

In stillness, there is only the completely authentic expression of the Self in this moment. The expression of an older body will be different from the expression of a younger body. There are also differences according to social position, but none of that matters. It is all inessential.

Then does this illusionary self-image develop from a poor self-image to a better self-image?

As long as realization is incomplete, the illusion of an I who develops appears. Development can only exist out of comparison. If there is no comparison, development doesn't exist. Development is the comparison between a past image and a future image. Out of this comparison, the illusion of an I who develops appears. In reality, however, both images exist *now*, the past image as well as the future image. When there is the understanding that both images exist *now*, there can be no development from one image that exists now to another image that equally exists now, so there is no sense in talking about development. Yet, on a relative level, as long as realization is incomplete, there appears to be an I who develops.

Realization is touching stillness, and touching stillness is the end of development. I haven't heard of anybody experiencing development in meditation.

Does the mind develop?

The mind develops, but only as long as you believe in the reality of the mind.

* * *

Ramana Maharshi aroused hostility by just sitting there and doing nothing to alleviate the suffering of the world. Many western seekers thought he should go out and tell everyone to wake up and stop destroying the world. He did nothing. He just sat there, still, incredibly still. The power of this stillness went on developing in unforeseeable ways and made Satsang possible through further forms of the teacher. In Ramana, there was neither the thought that he should do something to save the world, nor the thought that he shouldn't do something to save the world. There simply was no thought at all. And when there is no thought, no idea, then what is right occurs, for it simply occurs out of the Self. It is divine action, impersonal action, not action arising out of a *thinking mind* that wants to imitate divinity.

* * *

Bliss is *That* which is the source of every state. It is
That out of which the body comes into existence, *That* out of
which these words appear. It is the *One* who speaks and
the *one* who listens; the *One* out of whom in this moment
everything comes into being. *That* is the source. It is
consciousness itself. And this consciousness is complete in
this moment. It needs not to be searched for; it needs not to
be found. It has been realized long ago. You need to be
liberated from the ignorance that consciousness is
something that will be realized sometime in the future.

You are already your*Self*, and you are already the
completeness of your*Self*. If you really allow this
completeness of the moment, everything is possible,
everything becomes perfectly clear. The problems that
burden you, which never arise out of this moment,
dissolve. It seems to be a miracle, but it is perfectly natural.
It is nothing but the readiness to spend one moment in
peace.

The mystery of Being reveals itself to you as
your*Self*. This revelation cannot be put in words. It cannot
be understood by the mind. It cannot be understood,
period. Consciousness is endless. All organisms appear in
you. Everything is filled and pervaded by *you*.
Consciousness is empty. It is nothing. When you turn
toward it, it will absorb all ignorance and the
misunderstanding that there has ever been anything other
than *that*. It will absorb any thought, any I-thought, any
appearance, until you totally realize: "There is only *this* and
nothing else." In this consciousness, all searching stops, for
the search itself is just a thought, and that thought sinks
back into consciousness.

* * *

It is a mystery that you overlook what is most obvious, the obviousness of yourSelf untouched by forms, feelings, or thoughts. The complete awareness of consciousness ends the story of suffering that is not even "yours." Whatever happens in this process called evolution, there is something that remains untouched by it.

The mind is exclusively occupied with what happens in evolution and gives arbitrary meaning to it. Diving into evolution happens through the instrument of thought. Without thought, it is not possible to dive into evolution. If you are completely still for one single moment, if thought calms down in total consciousness for just one moment, evolution is interrupted. In that, everything you have identified as *I* is interrupted. It is like a second of sleep. But this second of sleep is a moment of being totally awake.

* * *

When the mind goes inside into stillness and meets the Self, does that express itself as bliss?

Yes, but bliss is not a feeling. Bliss expresses itself in the "bliss of bliss." It is not the blissfulness that appears as a feeling. The "feeling" of blissfulness is very often confused with bliss itself. Feelings come and go. The feeling of blissfulness also comes and goes.

Many people search for bliss and are even addicted to it because it feels so good. But the bliss that you experience in the state of pure Being is Itself not a state but *That* out of which all states arise. This true bliss is the background of any experience, no matter whether it is ordinary or extraordinary. It is never absent. The feeling of blissfulness, however, can be absent and can become stronger or weaker.

Many search for feelings of bliss and therefore travel to India or other sacred places. because this feeling is taken for love. Yet the feeling of bliss is not love itself; it arises out of love. Love is not a feeling. Feelings of love arise *out* of love, but love itself is not a feeling. If love were a feeling, it would be very limited.

The *thinking mind* specializes in splitting off feelings to such an extreme that it then searches for these feelings and even comes to Darshan to experience a particular feeling. There is a possibility that this expectation will not be met. Feelings are like the weather, and the weather changes continually.

How do you define the Self? The way I understood you, it belongs to the impersonal. Until now, I always learned and believed that self was part of the personal.

What is personal?

To my understanding, self is the part that contains the emotions, the part that isn't enlightened.

That is what I call the *I*. The reason why Ramana substituted the expression of "Self" for "God" was to point to the fact that the Self is not to be found outside oneself. The divine Self and Divinity are one and the same. The *I* arises out of the Self, and it arises *now*, not in evolution. Forget about evolution. Evolution is based on belief, the belief that you were ever born.

Everything you believe you have ever experienced is only your interpretation. Your whole personality is based on indirect experience, not direct experience. If all your interpretations are no longer here in this moment, what remains of this entire personality? What remains of the whole identity of a somebody of a certain age and gender? *It* remains. To surrender to this *It* is Satsang. And surrender can only happen when thinking stops.

Allow this experience for just five seconds. That is the unknown in which nothing known can be measured on some scale—no diagram, no structure, and no concept—nothing that could describe this experience. Everybody has this experience every moment. That is the truth. Only humans deny this experience. They deny it because, as I said before, they are simply looking somewhere else.

* * *

A little while ago, you called the Self the source, the origin. My question is: Why does this Self exist at all? Does it exist out of itself? What is the reason for the existence of this origin? Did it start somewhere or was it just suddenly here?

The direct experience of the Self shows that there is no origin for the Self. There cannot be any origin for the origin; otherwise, it wouldn't be the origin. And experience shows that this Self, this total awareness that exists in this moment, has no beginning and no end.

The mind thinks in the dimensions of beginning and end, right and wrong, understanding and not understanding, knowing and not knowing, and in the normal state of man, this mind doesn't find any rest. The mind continually holds on to something, it believes that it knows or understands something; or the other way around, believes that it doesn't know or understand anything. Thus, it never reaches this point in the middle of which I speak.

In Satsang, it is necessary to sink into the direct experience of the Self. Source, origin, and Self are just words. In any case, it is *That* which you *are*. It is your*Self* and it is not confined to the body. It is *That* out of which the body exists. The body is *in* your*Self*. *You* are not in a body; your body is *in* your*Self*.

* * *

When you cling to what arises, you cling to what dies, for all that arises is already dying in the moment of its arising. Through the great illusion of time, totally subjective perceptions of rapidity and slowness come into existence. The Self, however, does not arise. The Self *is*. The body arises, thoughts arise, feelings arise. The whole world arises in this moment. This arising, however, is not available to your perception because the vibration is too fast. Similar to the way the images on your television are created, the whole world and what arises in this moment is created, and in that same split-second, everything collapses, dies, and is immediately created again. It happens so fast that it seems to be out of the realm of your momentary perception. A vibration is created that appears to have continuity, but it is only an appearance.

And the mind that clings to what arises does not recognize its own origin. Out of the clinging to what arises, fear of loss and dying are born, and that fear is justified, for what arises will, in fact, immediately die again. What remains is *you*.

* * *

What is Truth?

Basically, I can only answer that question by describing what Truth is not. Truth is nothing you can seize by thought, as you have tried until now. Truth is nothing you can perceive by the five senses, or supernatural senses, or by any sense at all. Truth is not an object. So, if you cannot seize Truth, neither by the senses nor by thought, what remains?

Being.

Suchness Without Meaning

Most people need some preparation for the question "Who Am I?" by dealing with what they are not. This preparation is therapy. Therapy and esoteric teachings deal with what you are not. Most people think that when they are in therapy, they are dealing with themselves, but this is indeed a gross misunderstanding. Therapy is not dealing with yourself. Therapy deals exclusively with what you are not. And this is beneficial at a certain stage. It relaxes the Not-Self.

* * *

I do things like therapy or have a horoscope made to find out what is hidden behind my grief.

Normally, when you have some negative emotional experience such as pain, grief, or rage, the mind slips some story over it, some drama, and gives it a meaning that it does not have in truth. Nothing, in reality, has the meaning that the mind gives it. In reality, no meaning exists.

Esoteric teaching goes as far as meaning goes. It gives meaning to the things that the mind, still numb and ignorant, was not ready to give. As a transitory stage, it can be important to recognize the hidden meaning behind things, but ultimately, it is necessary to go deeper than meaning, to go *into this moment*. Meaning is never in this moment. Meaning always involves a story, a spiritual story, a psychological story, or whatever concepts are brought up from the past to explain something. The result is nothing but a system of thought that is never able to recognize *That* which is deeper than thought, *That* which you *are*.

* * *

Every action simply happens. There is no meaning to its happening, and neither is there any meaning to how it happens. It just happens. When you reject all interpretations of right and wrong, whether justified by the noblest therapeutic or spiritual teachings, then you are ready to realize *suchness*. Suchness cannot be understood by the mind. Zen teachers of all generations spent their lives passing on to their students this (non)-teaching of suchness. As described in Zen, suchness is, "the meadows are green" and "the flowers are red."

There are many positive approaches given in psychology and esoteric teachings to awaken from this numbness in which the mind dwells, this numbness that only pretends to be without meaning. This is not real meaninglessness. It is just numbness. To wake up from this numbness, it can be momentarily helpful to ask for meaning. That is what esoteric teachings do. They try to discover the hidden meaning behind things. However, the mind that is occupied with esoteric teachings believes that this hidden meaning has some reality. It doesn't have any reality. It is just a landing of understanding. Where esoteric teachings come to an end, Zen begins. The teachings of Zen begin with the true realization of the meaninglessness of all objects.

If there is a story of a person, there must be suffering. In meaninglessness, there is no suffering. Suffering comes into existence simply by your attaching some kind of meaning to yourself, but what you believe yourself to be has no inherent meaning. When you realize the meaninglessness of Being, you are free. Any presumption of how things should happen, or what it means if they do not happen the way you believe they should, is the meaning I speak of.

For instance, if, as a therapist, clients suddenly stop coming, you might think, "Oh, my God, what have I done wrong?" Nothing! Clients have stopped coming; that is all. As long as you cling to any meaning, things will indeed *have* a meaning. What you may not recognize in this moment is that the meaning you put to things is a self-fulfilling prophecy. In reality, these things don't have any meaning at all. Go deeper than meaning. Meaninglessness cannot be practiced. It is recognized in stillness.

Meaning has to do with the questions, "How?" "Why?" Satsang is the question, *"Who?"* After the question of *who* has been answered, *how* no longer matters.

Free of Vice, Free of Virtue

Are there practical techniques to do or not do certain things in order to gather energy for Self-realization?

I wouldn't say that any technique renders Self-realization possible.

Does anything render it more probable?

What facilitates realization is the relaxation of the mind. As Da Free John expressed it, when self-contraction diminishes, Self-inquiry may be more easily possible. But I wouldn't claim even that because relaxation can be used immediately to fall asleep again.

I always have trouble endorsing any prerequisites for realization. Yet, neither would I consider realization to be totally independent of a person's energy level. Carlos Castaneda's teacher, Don Juan, supposedly even claims that a person's story of suffering has to do exclusively with a lack of available energy. The *thinking mind* wastes life energy by not totally understanding and respecting its flow. "Accept what comes and reject what goes," was Papaji's teaching. The I, however, habitually"rejects what comes and accepts what goes." All energy, all longing, has to be made available toward the desire for liberation. In regards to the subject of virtue or merit, if you feel good living certain virtues, do them. If you don't feel good about it, don't.

Contradictory and opposing forces appear through every personality. One moment, softness appears, perhaps the next moment, hardness appears. One moment joy appears, and the next moment anger appears. To call these forces contradictory or opposite requires comparisons made by the mind. The moment you give up all comparisons and stay with the *suchness* of what is, whether that comparison is some notion of the last moment or some imagination of the next moment, then softness appears when softness appears, and hardness appears when hardness appears. Separation appears when separation appears, and union appears when union appears.

What happens when you give up every comparison, when you even give up the attempt to give a name to what appears?

Then only this moment is lived and I am totally Here, Now. The moment is simply the moment without any evaluation. It is as it is, and there are no longer any problems. Then everything can just be. But the moment one idealizes or compares from different time periods, there will always be a discrepancy.

Comparison is always a gateway to ignorance. There are two essential gateways to ignorance. One is comparison, and the other, evaluation. Both work together. In this moment, can you dive into the suchness of what is without any conceptualization, without any interpretation, without any thinking about it?

"Re-flecting" or "pre-conceiving" is always after or before, never *here*. When you are *here*, the forces that arise out of the spontaneous aliveness of this moment can live. If the impulse is strong enough, it will express itself. And if the impulse is not very strong, it will stay within and not express itself on the outside. There is no obligation to express something and there is no obligation to not express something. Then, whatever is expressed in life is no longer controlled by a personal *I*.

When the mind is caught up in comparison, seeing inconsistencies and contradictory forces, it can often seem frightening. They frighten the mind because the mind never completely accepts duality, and it never accepts both sides of duality equally. However, in the natural state of stillness, there is no urge or compulsion to obsessively express negative energies. But that doesn't mean they don't appear. The natural state has nothing to do with excluding the negative forces of the universe. It has nothing to do with excluding anything at all. The moment the compulsive identification with the I-thought drops away, it is totally natural to live your inherent goodness, for your nature is good without any concept of goodness or any idea of what it means to be good. Goodness is a natural manifestation of man or any being.

There is no commandment of virtuousness in the name of apparent spiritual correctness. If there is a "somebody" who has to do something in order to be good, there is a problem. If there is a "somebody" who has to do something in order to be bad, there is equally a problem. When you give up both sides of duality and fall through the middle into stillness where the pendulum neither swings in one direction nor the other, then this natural goodness of your being can shine through you in its simplicity.

It doesn't require any effort to be good. It is essential to understand that any effort to be good must be given up as well as any effort to be bad. All of that is just the basic movement of the pendulum of the mind. One movement of the pendulum is the effort to make oneself good, to elevate oneself, and then the pendulum swings in the other direction, to make oneself bad, to berate oneself. Both require effort, for both are artificial and do not relate to your true nature.

Give up any effort to become a better person. Give up any effort to become a worse person. Give up both these efforts. *That* which you are has nothing to do with any of that, and it is not touched by these attempts that are nothing but thoughts and imagination. How is it when the burden of this movement of the pendulum falls off your shoulders just for a moment, when any attempt to be somebody or to act in a certain manner falls away?

It's good. I feel relaxed.

Let everything fall away. It is all an unnecessary mental burden, misunderstandings that you carry around inside yourself.

*   *   *

How have your emotions changed? Do you actually no longer identify with them?

All feelings can be here.

You are just in this moment with them and don't think about them?

Feelings arise and burn away in consciousness the same way as thoughts arise and burn away in consciousness. Nothing keeps all of this together, no I, not even a soul, which also exists only in imagination. All that keeps this together is consciousness itself and consciousness itself is totally impersonal.

Then, do you experience something like indifference?

No, it is not indifference. It is equanimity. Are you aware of this distinction? The notion of indifference suggests some kind of distance, a hidden resignation, and is frequently just a reactive tendency of the mind. For instance, indifference often shows up on the spiritual path as an expression of frustration or a hidden attachment to death. In equanimity, there can be no real distance or anyone who could keep a distance, because there is no separation between *you* and *what is*. Authentic experience, without any attachment of an I, is serene.

*   *   *

All laws of morals and ethics have been created as a substitute by the *thinking mind* because the *Self* has seemingly been lost, one's true origin has been denied. And in this origin of consciousness, in No-Mind, there is no necessity to maintain any law. What morals imitate is totally natural to *Beingness* itself, and there is nobody who has to control this. There are neither morals nor anti-morals. Morality is an artificially created construct of thought. When action happens spontaneously out of the natural state of being, there is no possibility for any action to be either right or wrong, and consequently, there is no necessity to judge action. Who judges? How many priests are there whose entire teaching consists of giving new values to thinking, feeling and acting? All of this happens within the framework of an artificially created construct of thought. In the natural state, it is not necessary to distinguish right and wrong actions.

* * *

You once described something very paradoxical: One cannot search for God, but neither can one find God if one doesn't search. So I can't say: I don't need to do anything because I can't do anything anyway. On the one hand, this is true. On the other, however, it is not. I have to do what I believe needs to be done.

A master gave his student two instructions for his path: "First, know that all efforts to find God are in vain. Second, act as if you didn't know the first." You always do whatever it is you need to do, simply and clearly.

That is always the case anyway, whether I am realized or not.

What do you mean by that?

Simply that I have to be authentic in this moment. Is there any other way? If there is no duality, then neither are there any alternatives.

In the experience of duality, which is where the *thinking mind* lives, there are certainly alternatives. On a spiritual level, there is the necessity to discriminate between the voice of the heart and the voice of the mind. Apparent duality consists of the fact that there is an authentic voice and at the same time possibly an almost perfect copy of this voice, appearing then as temptation. It tempts you not to differentiate between them. It is solely your task to recognize the authentic voice and to act accordingly. That could be called the essence of spiritual "growth" and the task of the seeker.

Love Without Relationship

Can you say something about love?

How can I speak of love? I can only tell you what love is not. I would say that next to the concept of enlightenment, love is the most misunderstood concept, for love, as well as enlightenment, cannot be grasped by any concept.

What can I tell you about love that you won't make into a concept? Love is neither an emotion nor a feeling.

The other day an Osho disciple took my words in Darshan and said, "All you say sounds so intellectual, but I miss love!" I replied that love *is*, in this moment, and it is the love out of which Darshan occurs. Like many seekers, he had a sentimental concept of love, and this concept stood between him and the teacher, between him and *himSelf.* When the mind speaks of love, it is mostly speaking about sentimentality.

What you search for is that which does not pass. States pass and feelings pass. If love were a feeling, it would pass. Love can only be found in *That* which does not pass, and *That* which does not pass is nothing that can be perceived. It is *That* which perceives. And *That* which perceives is *That* which you *are.* And *That* which you are has no definable facets by which love can be confined.

Love has no polarity. It is nothing that can be described. Everything that comes out of the Self *is* love. A fit of anger can equally come out of the Self and that fit of anger equally occurs in love. In the moment that any concept, any past, or any future fall away, in that moment, love *is.*

How will you measure love? The moment you say, "Love looks like this but not like that," you've lost it.

There are many spiritual teachings about love. They teach how it is to be in love and how it is not to be in love; what love means, what love doesn't mean, and what love forbids. Those are only concepts about love, not *love itself.* There is no need for a teaching about love. All that is needed is the recognition of your true Self, and in this recognition, love is realized. Which form love will take, who knows?

* * *

What is the practical meaning of relationship? The relationship with other people, especially in everyday life, sets ever new challenges by which you can grow. In this way, it also can be seen as a model for one's relationship with God. How, for instance, can a man and woman both grow together spiritually?

This approach is too limited in its understanding. What is normally called a relationship with someone else is really a relationship with images that you then project onto so-called others. It anyway isn't a relationship within a really existing duality between "I" and the "other." It is a dualism within the *thinking mind*. Certain parts of this *thinking mind*, this false *I*, are split off, projected outward, and then appear as "outside." That, then, is called relationship. So, first of all, there is no true relationship between "you" and the "other."

What is called "growth," or the process of understanding, is that these reflections, which seemingly appear on the outside and originate in the *thinking mind*, are then understood and integrated in some way. These reflections originate in the shadow of the mind. Consequently, it is all a process taking place within the design of the *thinking mind*, within the illusion, but it doesn't touch reality.

When we speak in Satsang of the notion of partnered relationship on the level of Leela, the divine play, it is based on the presupposition that the *thinking mind* has been recognized for what it is. On this level, nothing takes place but the play of two arms of the Self, the original female force and the original male force, and these two forces play with each other. It is an experience of joy and beauty. There can also be friction between them and arguments can happen. Yet, in this authentic experience, there is no identification of an *I* as either man or woman. They are just forces of the Self, enjoying each other.

The notion of relationship always has to be applied to an apparent, unrealized *I*. What does relationship really mean anyway? It means that there is a "somebody" who relates. In other words, there is a subject and an object to which it relates. Who really relates to whom? Neither subject nor object can survive close self-examination. The deeper you investigate, the more this supposed relationship turns out to be a joke.

Eli Jaxon-Bear has reduced "relationship" to a simple common denominator, which, in my opinion, expresses everything. It's called, "Give me something I don't have."

To speak of relationship only makes sense as long as there is an *I* who believes there is something between who one is and life, whatever life is. Then it makes sense to approach relationship as a means to diminish the distance so that you can go into relationship totally. In total relationship, there is no longer any "I" who relates or any "you" to whom one is relating. The paradox is that by its own definition relationship means distance. Consequently, when a man has a "relationship" with a woman, this means distance. Out of that arises the ultimately fruitless attempt of the mind to overcome this distance by merging. First, the mind builds up distance through the concept of relationship, and then it tries to overcome this artificially created distance by the concept of closeness. This is the absurdity of the mind. First it creates obstacles, and then it tries to remove them. In reality, there is no distance, no closeness, and no relationship.

I don't speak of the notion of relationship as having any reality. Relationship only exists from mind to mind. The *thinking mind* is capable of making self-created images of itself appear as the supposed "other" on the outside. Any growth between people, couples, or beloveds is first of all a process of understanding within the *thinking mind* and has nothing to do with a relationship between one person and another person.

What I meant is that by living with someone else, certain challenges are created that can lead to the experience of no separate I.

What kind of challenges are those? Challenges arise out of mentally constructed preferences and dislikes. So, if your partner lives something on the apparent outside that contradicts the image you have of yourself, something that belongs to your set of dislikes and is outside the framework you've staked out for yourself, then it is exactly the kind of relationship of which I speak: A shadow of your false I-structure is projected outward, and then in some way or another resistance gets built up against that. This phenomenon of never-ending shadow boxing is what is normally called relationship.

When in a meditative state of mind, in the state of No-Mind, which is your natural state, things happen, there are really no challenges because you are with whatever happens, and there is neither movement against nor movement away from it. There simply is that which *is*.

But you are always presuming enlightenment. It is true that seen from your perspective, enlightenment, truth, or oneness is always here. But how does it work from the other side? How can two people work on themselves together, within their relationship, to fully realize this oneness?

The basic premise of your question is that there is somewhere "to get to." The moment you deal with these concepts of relationship from this level of understanding, you only create it as a reality. It is possible to bring this to consciousness within the relationship, but it is equally possible to immediately leave it because it does not correspond to *reality*. This *thinking mind* has the potential for ultimate recognition, and ultimate recognition is possible only in this moment.

What I am talking about is a totally radical approach, an approach that is ready to leave behind all relative levels of understanding and dive into the simplicity of reality. If you are willing to leave understanding for direct experience, this can only occur *now*. This willingness is what has distinguished the few from the masses, the few that were ready to fully face reality. It is an uncompromising willingness not to deal with all the different levels of the inessential. Quite a few spiritual seekers are occupied with seemingly very interesting levels of understanding. These are, however, nonessential. For instance, teachings about "man-woman" relationships.

You have to presume enlightenment, for enlightenment is the true experience. If you have no experience of enlightenment, you are not in reality, that's all. I have to presume enlightenment in our conversation because then I do nothing but presume reality. And how can I not presume anything but reality? That would be totally absurd. It is my concern to point to the exploration of your own authentic experience, and that is possible in this moment.

In reality, there is no relationship between me and any other. That is the truth. I can only speak about relationship on the level of small self-inquiry and the *thinking mind*. There, it makes sense to me.

The subject of projection is an absolutely essential subject in the investigation into the *thinking mind*, and relationship is marked exclusively by projection— inasmuch it makes sense to explore projections. But whenever we speak of relationship, we are starting from the concept of an uninvestigated *I* that relates to an uninvestigated *you*. All the teachings about good relationships have not recognized the level of true Self-inquiry, the possibility of a direct view of reality, as taught by Ramana Maharshi. They work exclusively within a mental construct and don't understand the possibility of a direct investigation into reality that leaves behind the constructs of the *thinking mind*. It is not possible for any *teaching* to ever leave this construct. Do you realize the absolute radicalness of this?

You have to be totally radical. Radical means, "at the roots" (lat. *Radix* = root). Freedom is radical, and you cannot compromise freedom in order to deal with certain limited levels of understanding just because you believe you are not ready for absolute understanding. You *are* ready! But if you *believe* that you are not ready, you are not. The *thinking mind* is a self-fulfilling prophecy, a phenomenon that continuously generates itself, that confirms itself and thus comes true. It generates itself and gives itself truth.

When you are in the direct experience of No-Mind, it doesn't matter whether you are with people or not. Either you are joyfully with people or you are joyfully alone. The *one* complete relationship, the relationship with the Self, is always here.

Growth, in the sense of sinking deeper into realization, can happen through anything, and other people are not necessarily needed as reflections. It's possible that no reflection whatsoever is needed from the outside. It is possible that this process is a purely internal process, totally separate from any outside reflection. It is possible as well that there are outside reflections that continue to support the process of sinking deeper and deeper, as for instance, a partnership. But to give importance to the concept of a relationship between "me" and "other" means to deny the *one* relationship.

But can't it be supportive when two people both get involved in finding the truth and help each other? Why are there so many problems when a woman, for instance, begins a search for truth and the man doesn't?

When you give up shadow boxing and pull back the attention normally directed to the outside, out of this total internalization that is no longer about "Give me something that I don't have," a seeming paradox occurs in which you no longer want anything from your partner. When you no longer want anything from your partner, only then is it possible to truly *be* with your partner and to touch what it means to be with your partner in the Self. Then the unfulfilled desires assigned to your partner are recognized as desires within the *thinking mind* merely projected onto your partner. In this way you avoid getting caught up again in this play of shadow boxing.

On the relative level, one can say that of course there can be mutual support. Whenever there is within you the genuine wish and the readiness to be in truth, this will be reflected on the outside. But neither does that have anything to do with a relationship in the absolute sense.

Yes, there can arise great beauty between lovers. The natural way to be continues to appear out of a not completely realized state as well, for instance in the way you are with your girlfriend. It appears in moments you laugh together, or perhaps in lovemaking, or in moments you meditate together. In these moments, the heart is simply with the heart, but in any case, these are states of no-thought, out of which can then be experienced what is permanent in realization.

* * *

What is the essence of love, and how is sexuality related to that?

This question can only be answered in relation to the one who asks the question. To answer the question in a general sense, I have to split the answer into two.

Sexuality is a double-edged sword that can be a celebration as well as be misused by searching for love in sexuality and confusing sexuality with love. It also is a double-edged sword because it reinforces the mind's tendency to identify with the body.

First of all, it is difficult for the mind to meditate when involved in sexuality because sexuality has the same effect as a drug. Sexuality *is* a drug. When you take a drug, the mind will have the tendency to direct the attention toward the "dust" that gets kicked up by the drug instead of meditating and being with the essential. If you take LSD, the dust consists of hallucinations, and if you use sexuality as a drug, the dust consists of all the side effects created in the body by the distribution of hormones. So much dust is kicked up by sexuality that the stimuli overwhelm the mind, and it loses the awareness of being beyond any boundaries of the body.

Satsang has nothing to do with any teaching on sexuality. To be in Satsang means to be beyond any teaching. Inasmuch, there is nothing to teach about sexuality that can be universally applied beyond the known facts of physical functioning. When a teacher makes a statement about sexuality as it relates to a certain questioner, there is the danger of drawing general conclusions about it. The validity of the statement relates to a certain moment and the particular person asking the question. It doesn't have any other value. One cannot make a concept out of it that sexuality is good or sexuality is bad. There are people who have tried to follow the ascetic path and who have failed. Others have tried to reach ultimate transcendence through physical union and this also did not work. As far as I can see, any path via sexuality has ultimately failed.

The mind following a spiritual path moves from materialism into spirituality. To leave behind materialism means to direct the attention away from matter and thus at the same time also away from the body. The body is not only an *expression* of matter, the body *is* matter. Yet the development from materialism to spirituality is in itself not true development. The misunderstandings and concepts, the beliefs and ideas of the mind, are just transposed to another level, the spiritual level. That, then, is called the spiritual path.

I see that for many seekers, who have turned away from material levels, there arises the problem of denying sexuality because it has been subjected to a noble pseudo-spiritual reformation. I see the great damage done by thousands of years of Christian conditioning through which sexuality has been condemned and put in opposition to holiness. This includes seekers from the West, who, it is true, don't call themselves Christian but who deeply and subconsciously cling to these collective beliefs and deny sexuality out of spiritual concepts. The United States is a good example of it. The founders of the United States were Puritans whose religious misunderstandings about asceticism and abstinence still poison the collective consciousness of the *thinking mind* that identifies itself as "American." It is also perceptible how much tension the minds of American seekers hold in this area. Even with most American spiritual teachers you can feel a slight bias when they are on the subject of sexuality. All of that has to be severed.

I don't say anything about how sexuality needs to be lived. I don't say that it has to be practiced or that it must not be practiced. I just see that the superficial concept among many spiritual seekers seems to be that sexuality must not be acted out, with the exception of certain New Age subcultures who practice Tantra, etc. Materialistic seekers, on the other hand, whose minds still cling to matter very strongly, seem to pursue sexuality as a means of defense against the recognition of their deep unhappiness.

What is the problem with sexuality? The problem is not in the body; the problem is in the mind. Exactly like all manifestations that come out of the Self, sexuality is an expression of celebration, an expression of the Self. To see any shade of negativity or positivity in what I say would already be a distortion because as I said before, there is ultimately as little to teach about sexuality as about any other subject.

Being in Satsang is the possibility of moving beyond teaching. It is the end of teaching. How many teachings are there and how many of those seemingly contradict each other? They don't contradict each other because they *truly* contradict each other. They contradict each other because they have been given from different levels of (limited) understanding. Does that answer your question?

About sexuality, yes, but not about love.

In its essence, sexuality is an expression of love and an expression of the nature of love. When sexuality is lived without any investment in what will come out of it, when it is lived spontaneously, as when anything else is lived spontaneously out of the moment, there is as little "danger" in sexuality as in anything else.

Especially in regards to sexuality it is important to be vigilant, on one side as well as the other. There have been many teachers who have recognized a problem with sexuality and who have then started to practice asceticism.

But that, too, can be a problem, for asceticism, as with anything else, can come out of an obsession of the mind. Yet asceticism can also be important in certain moments or certain phases. Only you can know that.

How do you understand asceticism?

Asceticism has nothing to do with an abstinence from "physical desires." So much unnecessary suffering has come from the misunderstanding that the spiritual path is all about sublimating "lower" physical desires. I know spiritual teachers who emphasize the alleged "sex trap" and point a finger of "spiritual correctness" at other teachers who have sex with students.

In my experience, I cannot ultimately confirm the importance of the subject of sexuality on the spiritual path. The only abstinence that is necessary is the abstinence of the I-thought. Here, the real core of the origin of asceticism is to be found. The I-thought, however, penetrates even into "physical thought" and seems to merge with the body. A seeker practicing Self-inquiry is able to recognize this. For the one who differentiates the *I* from the body, abstinence from sexuality is not necessary.

Gangaji says, however, that sexuality is not necessary.

That's absolutely correct, and I add that neither is abstinence from sexuality necessary.

* * *

Can you say something about loneliness and being alone?

The truth is there is no possibility of being lonely. In any moment the divine Self is present. To feel lonely you would have to deny this embrace with the Self. If people feel lonely, this is mostly a consequence of their frustrated desire for relationship. As long as this desire for relationship is seemingly fulfilled, it often covers the underlying feelings of loneliness. Only when you are, for instance, with a teacher and the habit of relationship is interrupted, can these underlying feelings revealed. In this case you are searching only for *one* relationship, the relationship with the Self. As long as you search for other relationships, you will feel lonely. For even if these relationships appear to make you momentarily happy, you will always have the experience of an underlying loneliness, for you know that finally the relationship will be lost, and this is your fear.

Ultimately, fulfillment will not be found in any relationship. The story about the soul mate is also a myth. That story is a widespread belief that sounds rather good at first, but if you examine it more closely, you recognize that even the relationship with a so-called soul mate is also transitory.

Therefore, don't look for supposed soul mates or any other relationships. Recognize in this moment that the true relationship with the Self *is*. You cannot believe it or think it. The only possibility of realizing it is to be still and listen inside.

No matter what you cling to, it is a distraction and a defense against recognizing the truth of your*Self*. What I have said about relationships is not only valid regarding relationships with people. To the mind, everything is an object. In its desires, the mind doesn't really distinguish between things and people. For the mind, there are only objects, and those objects are potentially capable of fulfilling its desires whether they are people, houses, or whatever.

Self-realizatin is about giving up the relationship with objects. In this world of illusion, you can play in any illusion as much as you want as long as it seems profitable to you. That much seems to be free. For the only freedom man has is the freedom to suffer. That is truly the only freedom he has.

When the mind attaches itself to an object, it is a waste of shakti, of life energy. What the mind normally and exclusively does is attach the shakti to objects. At first, it is to objects on the outside, houses, cars, matter, people; and then it is to objects on the inside, thoughts, feelings, body sensations, images, energy, light, whatever kind of internal phenomena. Again and again, the same consequences arise: attachment, clinging, relationship, prison.

Discover what it is like not to attach yourself to anything, to no longer have to attach yourself and cling to any phenomenon because you think that if you let go, you will die. Give up all attachment to phenomena and see what happens. What you imagine happens isn't what happens, neither in the positive nor the negative. You also have to give up the attachment to these imaginations. You need no relationship with any object.

Recognize, who you *are*. You are completely alone, and every relationship to an object deceives you about your being alone. This aloneness that opens up is not loneliness. It is not depressive. Only *one* single relationship truly exists, and that is the relationship between you and the Self, a relationship without any relationship.

You are alone in formless consciousness, in That which does not manifest. And you are also alone in That which manifests as consciousness in form. Any idea of relationship is a deception, a running away from the experience of loneliness that is always just underneath it.

And underneath loneliness is (l)one-liness, the stillness of the Self.

* * *

What do you mean when you say, "When two people marry, the Self marries."

To me, in its essence, marriage is an act of true love, not an act of conditioned love. Neither is it the attachment to another person. A connection between two people can never bring true fulfillment as long as there is a relationship between them. Who relates to whom? Who am *I* and who are *you?*

Unfortunately, all too often the desire for marriage does not arise out of the joy of being, which does not require any fulfillment because it is already fulfilled in itself. The desire for marriage most often arises out of some idea of deficiency. As long as I feel this deficiency of being, I believe that somebody can fill the hole of this deficiency. "Give me what I don't have" is the creed of any relationship. This is conditioned, conventional marriage, and it is, unfortunately, the usual state of marriage. Naturally, to recognize that this search remains unfulfilled, even in marriage, is an essential step toward true fulfillment.

A man does not need a woman to be whole and a woman does not need a man to be whole. These concepts imparted by many teachings do not originate in Self-inquiry; they originate in the mind. If marriage took place in the mutual promise of Self-inquiry, it would be an act of fulfillment. In an act of fulfillment, paradoxically, there is no need to keep up the connection. If it is destined to continue, *Being* will keep up the connection.

There is also, of course, the fairy tale that marriage is forever. Marriage is as transitory as anything else arising out of the Self. Who can say how long the connection between two people is to continue? In the normal state of the mind, which maintains its existence through I-based thought, almost all actions arise out of some kind of deficiency, either openly or subversively.

The essence of marriage is a celebration of Self-Love, a celebration of Being in Love. Love without relationship. This apparent deficiency of Being from which everybody suffers cannot be filled by anything at all. No action in the world could in any way compensate for this assumed deficiency of Being. Only the pure realization, the pure recognition of who one really is redeems you from this dream that there is in any way some deficiency of Being.

* * *

What is love, really?

In Advaita, the teaching of non-duality, little is said about love. The reason is that anything connected with the notion of love has nothing to do with love or has to do as much or as little with love as everything else. What the mind takes for love is hormone release. No concept of love could be understood by the mind. As long as there is the slightest idea of what Love is, there is also an idea of what Love is not, or, more truthfully, what Love is not allowed to be. Love is that there is peace, and Love is that wars are waged.

I could tell you a lot about what love is not. It does not mean being just a certain way. Love cannot be touched by any idea. There is no one more or less loving than anyone else. Love has nothing to do with anything belonging to the personality. There is nothing individual about love. It has nothing to do with relationship. Everything that arises, arises out of love.

Does this mean that if a man and a woman are in love with each other, it is not really love?

The difference between "I love" and "I love you" is essential. The ego only understands love in relationship with an object. In the connection between man and woman, the flame of love is kindled. But this fire, which in truth is the fire of love for the divine beloved, unfortunately and all too often is not recognized. Then love becomes a possession of the ego.

The ego wants *to have* love and therefore it needs an object. Thus, the partner becomes the beloved object that then has to be possessed. The ego then calls it, "I love you." Remove the "you" from the "I love" and love is set free. Then you see that you can also lose the "you," but you cannot lose love itself.

You cannot love "another." If you believe you have to love another person, then you also have to make a strenuous effort. Then you are once again busy "pushing the car downhill."

In stillness, you *are*. Out of this stillness, love appears on its own. This does not necessarily mean, as the mind would interpret it, that you will be loved for it, because being in the *truth* of love naturally confronts all *notions* of love. This, the mind doesn't always appreciate. Love is. Love works.

Somebody once said that to live on a daily basis with a spiritual master as your partner is like getting a wet towel in the face. There is no longer anything to hide and nothing to pretend.

When there is surrender to the heart, there is great simplicity. There is a deep experience of beauty. The classical defense mechanisms that work in a "normal" relationship just don't work anymore. The universe has created relationship in a way that the mind of the one partner hooks exactly into the defense mechanisms of the other partner.

What is usually called relationship is a harmonious interplay between neuroses. Harmonious inasmuch as the neuroses always hook perfectly into each other and intertwine. Within this interconnection there is no possibility of finding clarity. As I said before, the relationship between "I" and "you" is nothing but the relationship between an I-concept and a projected you-concept. However, when the teacher doesn't take personally what is projected onto him and remains in stillness as a witness, the I/you play of the mind can no longer function. The partner's mind is thrown back onto himself, and this can temporarily be very uncomfortable.

* * *

A common psychological concept is that your partner is a mirror for you. What do you mean when you say the mirror also has to be destroyed?

Projections inevitably arise as a result of the identification with being a woman or a man, and the primordial force of the opposite gender is projected onto the other sex. These projections initially simulate a relationship.

Actually, the woman is no mirror for the man or vice versa when there is no longer anyone to look into the mirror. The reality of the mirror is perpetuated by the seer, who is continuously filling the mirror with the contents of his mind. When the attention is consciously withdrawn, the mirror breaks. This is what Poonjaji was pointing to when he said that finally, the mirror itself has to be destroyed.

I don't understand.

At that point, you are no longer looking into the mirror but into the one who looks. As long as you are looking into a mirror, you will obviously see reflections. As you look into the mirror, quite a lot can be understood, unconsciously at first and then more consciously with the help of psychological and metaphysical techniques. But all of this is still happening within the structures of ideas and thus within illusion. Not only is *what* you see in the mirror an insubstantial creation of the *thinking mind* but the mirror itself is also. There is the possibility of no longer looking into the mirror but rather seeing the one who sees. Then the mirror is no longer required.

Because you recognize yourself in the other?

No. The attempt to recognize yourself in the other is still looking into the mirror. I am not speaking about looking in the sense of looking *at* something. If there is looking at, there is "somebody" who looks and "something" looked at. This is duality. In the pure seeing of *That-Which-Is*, there is neither "somebody" who sees nor "something" seen. It is even simpler than the act of seeing. The recognition that the "other" is also *That-Which-Is*, is not a process or consequence of seeing but is contained in every natural moment of perception and doesn't require seeing as a process in time and space nor any conscious or unconscious effort.

Through the diversity of nature, we find ourselves in a house of mirrors where reflections on the inside and reflections on the outside first make recognition possible. Initially, reflections on the outside seem much more important, but as a mind matures, reflections on the inside become more fully usable. Ultimately, a mature mind that has turned inward and drawn the attention back from the outside world and thus from the partner as well, (which, by the way, doesn't mean that one is no longer close with the partner,) can immediately discern authentic inner reflections from false inner reflections. In this case, a purely inner process can take place without reflections on the outside being necessary.

* * *

Your mother, your father, and your siblings are not realized. They are not in touch with who you really are. How is your relationship with them? Do you sometimes feel pain or compassion?

From my point of view, there is only one single relationship and that is the only relationship you should seek. To seek other relationships, no matter whether they appear as "family" or as "partner," which are the main possibilities, is a dissipation from attention the truth. There is only one single relationship and that is the relationship with the *Self*. That is the only relationship into which you can ever really enter. What we call relationship with the family or relationship with the child is mostly a construct made of sentimentality, fears of loss, and the ego's claim to ownership. This construct of sentimentality has to be broken. In other words, I don't have a deep relationship with the person who calls herself my sister just because she is my sister, because "being a sister" is just a concept. There is a natural attraction between people who have grown up in physical closeness and relatedness, yet ultimately I would refuse every concept about it or any significance given to it.

The search for relationship is actually only about finding contact with the Self. Whenever you don't find this contact through another person, the connection with that person becomes nonessential, no matter whether it is your father or the postman that comes every morning. It ultimately doesn't matter who it is, for you live in connection with the Self and you see that where the Self shines through in its purity, there you are. That is your true family. The spiritual family is the true family. Only here is true meeting possible: from Heart to Heart, from Self to Self.

* * *

It seems that the "I," otherwise known as "the mind," splits off everything it doesn't want and takes on the form of other people. I see myself sitting here in a thousand different postures, both guilty and good, and I notice again and again, "That's me, that's me." There are a hundred "you's" in a single moment.

It is exactly like that. Creating a "you" seems to be the way out of the unbearable.

Somebody inside says "you" instead of "I" and because of this, everything belonging to the "you" is identified as separate. This seems outrageous.

The "me and you" game is the favorite game of society. "You" is a trick the mind creates so as not to become aware of itself. To be occupied with the "you" leads away from the essential. What I mean by "you" is everything you take for other people, equally for those you "love" and those you "hate." And the "you" takes on even more subtle disguises that get split off internally. Consequently, the you is not only "other people," but the you happens within yourself, as well in the form of culprit/victim dialogs, which are nothing more than subtle expressions of the same "me and you" game that usually takes place on the "outside." Sometimes it is expressed outwardly and sometimes it isn't, but it is the same game of "me and you."

You have already noticed that whenever you play this "me and you" game, you cannot identify with both parties at the same time. It is like one of those picture puzzles where two images are contained within the picture but you can't see them both at the same time. Your perception can only switch back and forth from one to the other. Every "you" is a split off from "me," a me that you reject and that you then project out into the world in order to fight against it more or less successfully.

So that I can say, "That's not me"?

Yes, and then the time is spent going on about the stories of these me's and you's and discussing it all thoroughly in order to not let the essential arise. It could become dangerous. Better to spend time with "me and you" stories.

The question of "who" becomes more and more obvious. Who is actually directing all of this? If there are nothing but "you's" here, who, then, is me?

This is an essential question. I would say it is the only question that pertains to Satsang.

This has to be the only important question, for I notice that quite a lot of you-stories arise whenever this question appears.

As soon as you recognize this mechanism, you can take it as a signal to return to the essential; meaning, to return to the question, "Who am I?" Who is the creator of this story? Who is the creator of me and you? Return to the creator. What people think of as relationship is a "you and me" story endlessly flogged to death. When you are really ready to go deeper with the question "Who am I?" you will realize that there is no longer any necessity for these stories. It becomes incredibly boring to go on expressing these stories because they are all the same old stories over and over again. The mind is like an old record that got stuck in a groove. Out of the 60,000 thoughts that are thought each day, eighty percent have been thought before. That's 60,000 multiplied by 365 days per year multiplied by 75 years . . . well, you do the math.

Also suffering seems "you" — you, Africa; you, Third World; you, my partner; you-thoughts, and you-feelings. Suffering always has to do with "you." As long as suffering is about the "you," the "me" is not ready to take responsibility for it entirely. Only out of this total responsibility is liberation possible.

"You" is created by the hidden desires of "me." Hidden desires that are not aware of themselves are what creates the "you" and what creates a relationship with the "you." For this reason, open relationships do not exist. Every relationship with "who" or "what" has hidden factors. The true motivations are cloaked. This is not an open relationship. The term, "open relationship," is a contradiction in itself. "Open relationship" would signify that the "me" is realized and then, correspondingly, the "you" is realized. The moment the "me" is realized, the "you" is realized, and when the "me" is realized, there is no longer "relationship."

* * *

There are situations with other people, for instance with my parents, in which old patterns of mind get triggered. It is like an old movie that is being played. Yet I no longer have the impression that the old patterns are imposed on me. They are like vague memories, while I know about the true state.

Yes. The moment you meet "other people," you very often meet images of your own mind, and this is why the same old temptations come into play. But without temptation, there also wouldn't be recognition.

What temptation?

The temptation of an unfulfilled desire directed outward. For instance, the desire to be understood or to finally be recognized by another, and this temptation keeps pulling you up to the surface, away from the realization of emptiness, away from the depths of the ocean so that attention is now directed toward the waves on the surface of the ocean. Be aware of this temptation and aware of its consequences, because in this moment, it seems to you as if you are split. There is a split into "me" and "the other." This process inevitably happens in thought, and you are perhaps not aware of its full scale. Something really fundamental happens the moment you meet with other people. For some people, this energetic split is particularly strong.

When I feel expectations directed toward me as to how to be or behave, this childlike aspect of conditioning arises where I automatically want to fulfill these expectations. That's why I mention my parents.

Others never direct expectations towards you. They first appear within yourself in the form of thoughts. These expectations are thoughts; thoughts projected outwardly that then return. They are always your own thoughts. You stay entangled in these thoughts rather than falling deeper inside. Expectations reveal that in this moment you want something other than the freedom of your soul.

*   *   *   *

Why do I find it difficult to be clear with my partner, to express things clearly and not deceive him?

Being clear with a partner is not the essential point. In what you call partnership or relationship, you will see that thinking, acting, and feeling are continuously directed outward with the tendency to fixate on the partner or some other exterior reference point. You know this tendency because it is a basic tendency of the *thinking mind.* In a partnership, this tendency is hugely reinforced because the partner offers him or herself and is at your disposal as a permanent screen for your projections. It is not your job to disillusion your partner; it is your task to disillusion yourself.

When you yourself are ready to explore the truth, whatever the cost, and when you feel this maturity in yourself to rest in the center of your being, then it is your job to be true to that. It is not your job to control how much of it gets through to the outside, and what that looks like, or even to ask questions about it. When you are ready to be still in order to liberate yourself from all the garbage made of thoughts and emotions that inevitably reappear, when you are able to let it go again and again and just stay with yourself instead of continuing to project it onto the partner, then actions happen that are no longer subject to your control. To find the right action towards your partner is not the point. The partner is no longer the reference point.

The paradox is that ultimately, it is only out of this total retreat that true closeness can arise. The more you reach for something on the outside, the less closeness will be possible. This is my experience. Not only does it apply to a partnership, it applies to everything else as well. In this dilemma of unfulfilled desires that arise out of a beggar's mentality, out of insatiable greed, the more you follow these wishes and start reaching, the less closeness to the Self is available to you. Closeness cannot be attained by techniques. Closeness to other people arises naturally out of Being.

* * *

When I meet someone to whom I feel attracted, there arises a feeling of deep recognition and seeing myself.

Is it like a premonition of seeing yourself?

Yes, it feels like that sometimes, but it is like I somehow need someone else in order to see myself.

You feel you need to look into the mirror in order to see yourself. When you look into a clean mirror, you don't see distortions of yourself, you see yourself in your pure form. However, you are still confusing the mirror with the

Self. Remember, it is still just a mirror, and this mirror doesn't show anything outside yourself, even if at first the mirror seems to be outside yourself. Then, this warm feeling that arises is very beautiful and doesn't create any suffering.

The problem arises the moment something is done with the feeling, when the feeling gets interpreted as, "Ah, this signifies that, . . ." and "that now means this, . . ." and "hopefully this will turn into that, . . ." but, "please not that way," etc. The problem arises the moment you try to fit the beauty of this authentic feeling into some kind of story in the form of meaning and desires. The result will be that this feeling gets so distorted it will begin to show up as suffering. This originally warm feeling turns into a claim of ownership, arising out of a perceived self-deficiency that doesn't really exist. If you have the feeling there is some kind of deficiency in you, you cannot overcome it by pretending it is not there. Positive thinking will not affect this deficiency. As long as you believe in deficiency or doubt deficiency or try to overcome it psychologically or spiritually, you will fool yourself and the deficiency will appear to be there anyway. But you can explore whether this deficiency is the truth of yourself.

I do feel a deficiency in myself.

This deficiency is your lie. It is the lie of your mind. You cannot overcome this lie. You can only *recognize* it *now*. Where is this deficiency? I don't see it. If you see it, please tell me where it is.

You don't see it?

I don't see it. You have to tell me where the deficiency is. When you look for it *directly*, where is it?

Look closely. Not outward, but inward. Be in meditation. Simply be with yourself. Where do you find it?

I don't feel any deficiency right now, but I suspect that if I were to live this awareness alone and not in relationship with anybody else, it would be very difficult for me to maintain this feeling of no deficiency. In such a union where you no longer feel any "other," relationship is no longer necessary, is it? I think I am afraid to be alone in such a union.

Every mind feels a deficiency, no matter how the mind behaves outwardly or whether the deficiency is compensated for or not. Every mind is based on deficiency, whether it appears outwardly self-confident or shy or strong or whatever. All of those qualities are manipulations of the mind. Every mind is based on deficiency, and every mind looks for relationship. The fact that it looks for relationship proves this deficiency, a deficiency that has neither been recognized as such nor explored in its essence. Many people who are not ready to go deeper actually land in the illusion of relationship only because they are afraid of being alone. But being alone is not what you conceive it to be.

The truth is, you are alone anyway. It makes no difference whether you look into one mirror or into a hundred mirrors. Even in a gallery of mirrors you are alone.

What we call relationship is one of the greatest sources of suffering in the world. Naturally, there are beautiful and ecstatic moments in relationship. There are moments that promise happiness. Otherwise, the mind wouldn't be so stupid as to get involved in it. Relationship or no relationship has nothing to do with how many mirrors you look in to, which means whether you are with other people or not. According to your natural disposition,

you socialize or you don't. Sometimes you are with a
partner, and sometimes you are not. When you are with a
partner, you enjoy it. When you are not with a partner, you
enjoy it as well. Do you understand? It has no significance.

Many misunderstand spirituality to be some kind of
prohibition of the "outside" world. At first, the mind
prohibits any real spirituality, because to the normal,
mundane mind, spirituality is dangerous. Once the mind
turns toward the spiritual path, then what happens?
Suddenly, everything else is prohibited. In other words,
nothing has changed. The mind hasn't learned anything. It
has just transferred its own limitations and prohibitions
onto another level. It has just shuffled the cards again, and
now the mundane is prohibited.

Nothing is prohibited nor not prohibited. As to the
question of right action, when you are in stillness you
know exactly which encounters with which persons
support you in the realization of yourself and which don't.
Especially in this phase, which I would call the phase of
vigilance, in which you are walking on razor's edge, it is
not that the encounter with certain old friends necessarily
supports you, as neither do certain rituals or habitual
spiritual practices necessarily support you.

It is possible that radical changes are required. Many
teachers, as well as myself, have passed through the most
radical changes in conditions and encounters with other
people. But again, the danger lies in making a concept out
of it, believing that because the Buddha left his wife, left his
family, left his castle, retreated into the woods and
meditated, that's what you have to do now too. That would
be pure imitation, pure falsification. Perhaps it has nothing
to do with what the teacher is telling you right now. The
true teacher is inside, alive now, only now.

Many people, when they talk about the Buddha and
take him for the teacher, mean something that is dead.

They can quote for you, "The Buddha said at that time, . ."
but the Buddha didn't say anything at that time. Either the
Buddha says something now, or the Buddha doesn't say
anything at all. The Self, the true teacher, talks to you now,
out of yourself, and not outside of yourself in the past.

It is quite natural to be in this love relationship that
you search for, for the love relationship that you really
search for is the love relationship with the true teacher,
your own Self.

* * *

If realization means to be alone, I don't want to be realized.

This fear has something to do with the original
misunderstanding of the female mind. If the mind is
identified with being a woman, it believes it is not complete
without a man. Then the worst fears can arise, but these
fears are not the truth of *what is*.

Question this fear. I am not saying to beat it to death
with thoughts. When I use the word "question," I don't
mean thought activity. I mean to check the reality of this
fear because the pain is created by a misunderstanding.

I understand the pain is there because I have believed in a lie.

Yes, the lie is that you *are* a woman. As long as you
are identified with being a woman, you will be subject to
this misunderstanding.

Being a woman or being a man are both concepts of
the mind. They don't exist in reality. No one is either man
or woman. But you can certainly find teachers who teach a
lot about what it means to be a woman or a man, about
how man and woman should behave towards each other,

what makes one a "wild man," what makes one a "powerful woman," whether a woman should emancipate herself or stay at home behind the stove. Satsang begins when you are ready to reject any concept about what it means to be a woman or a man. Then certain dynamics about being a woman or a man will naturally arise, but there is nothing to teach about it.

This feels incredibly liberating.

Every attribute bestowed on Being is arbitrarily created as a concept of the mind. When you have no concepts about being a woman or being a man, then you are ready to *be* what you *are*.

In the Flow of Being

Can I live without thoughts?

Only a minimum of thought is needed to organize the work that is being done. And if you believe that a state of no-thought is a state of numbness, you are wrong. On the contrary, it is a state in which true intelligence can unfold for the first time. Unfortunately, in our society, intelligence is defined as having to do with the *thinking mind,* but there is a deeper intelligence that is untouched by the usual notion of intelligence. It arises out of a state of mind without thoughts, a state of No-Mind. It is free and pure, original intelligence, impersonal intelligence, that works in the service of mankind in an unpredictable way. It does not correspond to any concept. It knows no morality but follows unknown laws of the heart. It is not fathomable by the thought-machine of the mind. Its laws cannot be understood; they can only be lived. It is possible that they are contradictory, but not necessarily contradictory to certain standards.

The state of No-Mind_makes life very simple: What needs to be done in any given moment is done. The whole system of the organism is left to Self-organization. To pick up a glass of water and drink from it, you do not need the thought, "I am thirsty." Everything happens on its own. By shifting your attention backward, you begin to have an idea of the origin, of the source that brings forth the impulse to reach out for the glass of water, and that source is not a thought. Any effort, any thought, can be abandoned.

I know that the mind holds an infinite number of "buts" and a tremendous number of conditions under which this could supposedly only be possible. If you want, you can examine the "buts" one after the other, or you can have the experience of simply dropping all the "buts" for a moment and surrender to stillness of mind. You can infinitely experience that impersonal *being*, rising out of this no-thought state of mind, is perfect and no doing is necessary to reach it. This is the original key.

All experiences gained on the spiritual path — exceptional experiences, paranormal experiences, physical experiences, or emotional experiences — are of limited value because they are transitory. But realization of your own inner stillness is everlasting. That which is transitory should not be in the center of your attention.

In this stillness, you are beyond worries, and neither are there problems to solve. For problems, in the sense of frictions and turmoil occurring in the course of this lifestream, are also solved without the thought-machine believing it is responsible or even capable of solving problems. Finally, all phenomena are realized to be natural, energetic, sometimes taking a disharmonious course and sometimes a harmonious one. There are no longer any concepts that things always have to run harmoniously. Why should existence exclude the occasionally disharmonious way of things? As soon as you have any idea, that is to say, as soon as you follow any thought about how it should be, how it could have been, how it has to be, or how it does not have to be, you've got a problem. *Existence* does not have this problem. In reality, this problem does not even exist. It is an artificial problem. In truth, nobody has a problem. All problems are artificially created. And if naturally occurring friction and disharmony are called "problem," this is totally different. If, for instance, two people come together and their personalities are contrary and friction occurs, that is not a problem. What happens is never the problem. It's the thoughts about what happens that are the problem.

When unpleasant things happen, for instance, when your house burns down, this certainly is very uncomfortable and not very pleasant, but it is not a problem. The house has simply burnt down, and whatever has to be done is what has to be done, for instance, find a new house. There are even worse losses, like the death of people who have become dear to you, or the sudden loss of a family member. Finally, there is the loss of your body. Eventually, you will lose everything, everything except your*Self*.

* * *

You have developed the neurotic habit of continually believing you have to do something in your thoughts, when in reality there is nothing to do. I keep comparing this to someone sitting in a boat, floating downstream and putting up an incredible amount of effort to paddle, while in reality nothing needs to be done.

It is ignorance about the nature of *Non-doing*. However, if you once touch Non-doing, if you once allow yourself to have the experience of Non-doing, then the experience of Non-doing can expand. Even if you fall back into an old tendency of having to do something, it does not matter. I am sure, once you have tasted it, you will prefer this state of letting go, of relaxation and opening into consciousness. In this opening of consciousness, uncomfortable material can also appear, but if you dwell in Non-doing, it has no significance.

Wanting to understand things, wanting to analyze things, giving things a meaning that sounds credible but does not correspond to reality, is continual *doing*. The first experience of Non-doing is a step toward letting go of the endless tendency to give meaning to all phenomena and a step toward giving up the never ending doubt.

When you touch Non-doing, you also touch the simplicity of being, and in this simplicity of being, the whole of Life takes place. Everything takes its course. It is, as Ramesh Balsekar calls it, the course of totality. There is nobody who should do something, everything *is being* done. The surprising thing is that everything that needs to be done gets done much more effectively because you are no longer continuously paddling, because as everybody knows, the stream flows downhill, not uphill. There is such an abundance of unnecessary movements of the mind, and these unnecessary movements of the mind consist of mental thoughts as well as of emotional thoughts. They create unnecessary resistance and friction losses. In this totally natural state of yourself, one-hundredth of your thoughts are enough to organize whatever needs to be organized.

* * *

What if you have an intention to accomplish some project? Isn't thought necessary for planning the project?

Ramesh Balsekar distinguishes the *working mind* from the *thinking mind*. The *working mind* is the Self in action. It is exclusively occupied with whatever work needs to be done. The *working mind* is the instrument of the Self so that whatever job is created, maintained, and destroyed is divine work. This *working mind* is not a personal identification. It does not create suffering. The *thinking mind*, however, is the deception that creates suffering.

Whenever something is planned, it can at any moment take a different turn from what was planned originally. The *working mind* is like a drop of water in this flow. The moment the flow is diverted, the water is also diverted. The moment something is planned and a certain direction is set, this can change completely in any given moment, for it is unknown how things will change. Things don't run positively in every moment according to your idea of "positive." In duality, it is not possible for everything to run in a positive way. This, too, is a hypocritical spiritual concept, that as long as there is positive thinking, things will run positively as well. But this is not true. Things will always run both positively and negatively. What does negative mean, anyway? It means nothing except that things that have been born must die.

The *working mind* works with the illusion of time without living in time. The only thing the *working mind* is occupied with is whatever has to be done in this moment, and it will accomplish this impeccably. Actions that are destined to be finished, are simply finished. Actions that are not destined to be finished, are not finished. Everything happens in consciousness in total clarity. There is no avoidance of actions, no avoidance of phenomena, no turning towards phenomena, and no turning away from phenomena. Yet, and this is a paradox that cannot be understood by the mind, battles can still arise because the falsity of the mind, when it is encountered, is not accepted.

Nothing can be said about how action happens through you. In any case, there is no trace of suffering in the planning of the *working mind*. The *working mind* is a self-organizing system that definitely also uses and integrates past experience into its work. All experiences that have been gained are used so that the work develops without your interference, without a "me" claiming it. Nobody is doing anything, yet everything is being done.

There is no disillusion because illusion no longer exists. And there is no one to either accept or not accept what happens. Find out *who* the *I* is. Ask yourself, "Who Am I?" Who is the I that acts, who is the I that does some kind of work?

* * *

According to my conditioning, I have to think first before I do something. How do I reconcile the idea that I have to be here, *and yet not think of being* here?

It really is as you say. The mind is conditioned to think first and then to act, and the belief that action arises out of thought is continually maintained. In an emergency situation, you don't think before you act because there is no time to think. The truth is that if you think before you act, then you are never *here,* because there is always some thought between you and the action, and that thought takes time. That is why, in the trance of thought, you are never *here.*

The amazing possibility is to see that in truth everything can happen out of a thoughtless state of mind with no *I* needed to control any of it. No-Mind opens the gate to a new dimension of intelligence in which thinking, feeling, and sensing arise from a deeper space inside you than the intellect. Be aware of your thoughts, and then notice how identified thinking makes you tense. Allow yourself to experience what happens when you just let the thoughts calm down, when you mentally relax. Let things come towards you, and deep down you will *know* that everything happens without any interference of an alleged "me" believing it is the one doing things in life. *You* actually don't do anything here; everything just happens. It is all the flow of totality, and you need not interfere. In reality, there is no one to interfere. The question is whether you have enough trust to experience what happens when you simply relax thought, when you need *nothing*, when there are no attempts to understand, no attempts to control, no fearful shrinking back, no resistance, and no doubt.

Once, I almost had a car accident on the highway when I hit a patch of black ice. I really experienced that some other kind of energy just took over the car without any thought on my part. It seemed technically impossible to prevent an accident, yet it was prevented.

And there was no thought in this moment?

No, another kind of energy took over.

Yes, this force that took over the car is the experience of divine energy.

I've had several such near-miss accidents that I couldn't have prevented by thought.

It is not that the divine energy takes over action in a given moment. It may appear that way, but it is not like that. The *thinking mind,* with its idea of being the doer, usually covers the divine energy. That's all. It's just like the clouds that "cover" the sky, but can the sky really be "covered"? The divine energy is always at play. The *thinking mind* just has certain concepts of what it means when divine energy acts and what it means when it doesn't act, what it looks like when it acts or doesn't act. The truth is that the divine force is acting in every moment, not just in an emergency situation. Sadly, it is only when the mind gets into such an unfortunate situation that physical life is endangered, t it is ready that it is ready to give up control and graciously leave the action to the divine energy, at least for a split second.

* * *

I am incarnated here in the physical world, and I also have to take care of my material needs. In my normal, everyday life, I have to pursue goals and make decisions throughout the entire day, and it is difficult for me to reconcile the spiritual world with the physical world.

When you are still, who takes care of you? Are you not taken care of when you are still? Are you not taken care of without your having to think about it? When you are still, is there anything that has to be done in order to *be*, to be in perfection, and to function perfectly well? When you are sitting here in this moment, you are in the *naturalness of being*, and in this naturalness, there is no necessity of making any effort to *be*.

You could say that for me to pick up this glass and drink out of it takes some physical effort, yet, paradoxically, it takes no effort at all. If you look closely, you see that it just happens. In exactly the same way I pick up this glass and drink out of it, everything happens. No *I* is required, no doing is required in order to make something happen that is already happening anyway.

The mind itself is a thought, an idea. The fear of not being able to survive is another idea. It also has nothing to do with you. It is just an idea that arises, no more and no less. It is meaningless. You don't return from the truth into some kind of everyday life. If you believe you return to everyday life, then you would have to leave reality. But you are *in* reality because you are *always* in reality. You are there *now*. When you refer to everyday life, you are not talking about *now*. You are talking about some kind of story taking place in your mind, and this story is nothing but thought. You don't live in everyday life. Nobody lives in everyday life. You live *now*. And this *now* does not have to be integrated into your idea of everyday life. Is it your experience, *now,* that there is no everyday life separate from *now*?

Now, yes.

What is the difference between now and *now*? If you check closely, is there any moment other than *now*?

Yes, that's just what I am doing. I am just checking to see, do I have to make a decision now?

Who makes any decision *now*? To let happen what is happening doesn't require any decision, any idea. A decision is an idea.

Being makes decisions on its own. *You* don't make the decisions. The one who believes itself to be making decisions is like the commentator of a football game who believes himself to be one of the players. The truth is that the game doesn't need him. His presence is completely insignificant to the game, the game of life — Leela. You live in the idea that you are a "someone" who makes decisions. The body doesn't make decisions, so who then is it that makes decisions? That there is a "someone" who makes decisions is your assumption, but if you will examine it, you will see that it is not your actual experience.

Being happens on its own. Everything has already been decided. It was decided a long time ago. This is not a form of fatalism, for fatalism is also just a concept of the mind. Fatalism is resignation. *Being* is beyond the polarity of fatalism or free will. It is neither one nor the other. You just *are*. And when you *are*, Being makes decisions. Decisions come to you, and you need not do anything. You are still, simply still, and all decisions come to you.

Imagine that there is a pilot (the *thinking mind*), believing him or herself to be flying this plane (the individual), and suddenly the pilot realizes, "The plane flies by itself!" There is no necessity to steer a plane that flies by itself. When the pilot then dissolves into *nothing*, he has always been nothing, but we pretend he is dissolving into nothing now, then there may be certain mechanical problems, which are, however, transitory.

Particularly problems with landing.

Yes, there can be problems when it comes to managing certain functions of the plane, but you don't have to do anything about it. That passes too. When the plane realizes itself as an object flying on its own, although in truth, it is no object at all, the result is complete clarity, complete transparency in everything. In every action, on every level of phenomena, there is complete stillness. The idea that as much movement as possible also creates as much as possible is an outdated idea.

You can be doing a lot of things and still be very indolent. One of the characteristics of indolence is that the body-mind works a lot, is in a lot of unnecessary motion. A lot of work may get accomplished, but only very little on the essential.

I like to use the comparison between lions and sheep. Sheep spend the whole day eating grass and are still not satisfied, while lions just lie around in the sun for twenty hours, dozing away. In the remaining four hours, they hunt with complete presence.

A problem can only arise in thought. For instance, in a circumstance in which it's not possible to do a certain thing, the idea can arise, "But I should!" You shouldn't at all. It is just your habit to believe that you have to do certain things in certain moments. In pure Being, everything is new. Everything is different. More is managed, not less. The *working mind* that works in the realization of itself, out of the essence of stillness, works clearly and effectively on what is essential.

* * *

When you have examined something for yourself and found the truth, do you then always take the path of truth?

It is not that there is a "person," in the sense of an "I" who examines. Incomprehensibly, it is *consciousness* that examines itself, that differentiates itself between the genuineness and falseness that also arise out of consciousness. Yet, it is falseness that creates suffering, and suffering is there to render realization possible. In this realization, the only possibility is to be in truth. There is no decision to follow truth or not to follow truth. In the stillness of yourself, in the state of No-Mind, in the natural state in which you *are* what you have always been, what you are *now,* and what you will always *be,* there is no possibility of not being in truth. The seeming possibility of not being in truth can only exist in thought.

It is possible to be with everything that arises, the good as well as the bad, the positive as well as the negative, without *trying* to be a good person or a bad person. The mind, in its efforting, continually swings to and fro between these two possibilities. You try to be good, but that takes effort, so sooner or later there is inevitably a turn and you realize that actually, you are bad. Then you try to pull yourself up again, try to make up for it, and so you go on swinging back and forth between both these two polarities. Sometimes a phase lasts for a lifetime, sometimes for a minute.

What if you neither try to be good or bad, if you simply *are* with what *is*, without identifying with what arises? When a feeling arises that doesn't please you, like for instance envy or jealousy, you can witness it without touching it, without doing anything. You don't give it a thought, a meaning. You witness, in complete consciousness, how it burns away, and it will burn away. *Everything burns away in consciousness.* This is the incredible possibility of which the mind can have no idea. In every situation, it is possible to witness everything that arises without touching it. And it doesn't take any effort. On the contrary, you have to summon effort to reach out for something and make a story out of it complete with pain and desperation and drama.

So the moment is just the moment.

Yes. The moment is the moment, and that is enough.

And if I have a desire to do something?
When you want to do something, there will be an impulse to pursue it without any doing on your part. When you are hungry, the body suddenly moves toward the refrigerator, opens the refrigerator, takes a piece of cheese out of it, closes it again, and eats the piece of cheese. But if the thought arises, "I am hungry," then you think you are the doer because you believe that you *are* the thought. But this thought is also just an instrument introduced by consciousness to transmit the impulse. You won't have the concept that a desire must not be fulfilled because it is prohibited or wrong. At the same time, there is no experience of a desire being unfulfilled.

Quite natural desires arise in every moment, but those desires are not the desires asserted by spiritual teachers to be the obstacles to enlightenment. The desires that have to be given up are the desires of the mind directed towards the future and coming from the past. But those desires have nothing to do with some playful wish that arises out of freedom in this spontaneous moment. For instance, the wish to play like a child, or the wish to just sit here in silence, or the wish to go to the movies, or the wish to have sex, or any wish that spontaneously arises in this moment. On the other hand, wishes that appear spontaneous can be, of course, subconsciously interwoven with a defense mechanism that is not at all spontaneous.

You have the experience that all of your unfulfilled desires are never really, ultimately fulfilled. This takes the search for happiness into eternity because you don't want to surrender to the fact that what you search for is already here in absolute completeness in this moment.

For instance, if you say, "Okay, Darshan is today, and I have to go there," but in the next moment, you suddenly don't feel like going, what is happening then?

It is not about somebody feeling or not feeling like doing something. This is ignorance. What happens, happens. The actions that are meant to be carried out, are carried out. There is no one separate from this action and the question of feeling or not feeling like doing something doesn't arise in the sense of, "I don't feel like doing it." When you no longer have the feeling of being separate from the action carried out, when you no longer believe in this, then it is quite natural for an impulse to arise and be brought to its completion. When it is time to come here for Darshan, I am not in the ice cream parlor eating ice cream, for this body-mind-mechanism, is self-organized. In this, it is perfect in all of its imperfection.

But in the moment a plan is made, it is a plan for something in the future. In the state you are talking about, I cannot imagine thinking about something three months in the future, or for that matter, the day after tomorrow.

You cannot imagine this because it is a contradiction. I would propose not even trying to imagine it, because it is a mysteriously self-regulated system that can even include illusions in its work without there being an *I* to suffer from it. There is no tension about something being planned for the future, and in spite of this, *you* remain completely in the only reality of this moment.

But you just said that you have to plan to give Darshan. You have to get involved in it. You have to say, "Okay, on such and such day, at such and such time, in such and such place, I have to give Darshan."

No, I don't *have* to give Darshan. Darshan is simply given. There is nobody outside myself who says, "You have to." There is no advice or punishment from God. Whatever happens, happens according to the *true* will. That's the way it is. And this will is in my *Self*.

So, I could say, "I want to give Darshan in this moment," but then I have no concept about how long this has to happen. In every moment, "I want" happens. And this, "I want," is "Your will be done." Your will is not separate from my will. The free will is not separate from God's will.

* * *

When I hear the mind speak of "non-doing," I recognize the taste of fatalism. And what I observe in most minds is the swing of a pendulum. On one end of the swing is a letting oneself go, either in resignation or in fatalism, and on the other end of the swing is a tense search. It is, as always, an approach to a paradox.

I can tell you not to do *anything*, but you have to be ready to do *everything*. And this readiness to do everything does not necessitate mental contraction. When you are not ready to do everything, nothing reveals itself to you, for he who doesn't search, doesn't find either. The understanding that "not searching" signifies that it is not necessary to do everything is a concept that puts you on a razor's edge.

There still seems to be a lot of emphasize on the will, and I can't deal with that.

Don't make the will your enemy, for the one who makes the will its enemy is also the will. This is absurd. Don't make anything within you an enemy. When you make something an enemy, you split it off, and in that moment, a senseless struggle arises. Even if it is in the name of enlightenment, it is senseless. Just relax.

A question that can lead you very deep is, "What is it that I really want?" The will itself is not the obstacle. The obstacle is the fact that you pursue levels and layers of unfulfilled needs that do not truly correspond with what you *really* want. This could also be called the false will. And this false will is nothing but your landing on a layer of the will. As Gangaji keeps emphasizing, "Never land anywhere, not even in enlightenment."

* * *

How can I best fulfill my task as a father?

The most simple answer is by being true to yourself. To be true to yourself means to let the *one* teacher appear, the Self, without assuming it to be an *I* that acts personally. What is a personally acting *I* anyway? Where is this *I* that identifies as a personal doer? Find it. As long as there is an *I* identified as a personal doer, suffering is brought into the world, and it doesn't matter whether these actions happen in the service of bad concepts or the service of good concepts, for it is not about bad or good ideals. It is about rejecting any concept, any thought, any I-thought, and remaining in the stillness of the impersonal state of No-Mind because the reality of yourself is impersonal. Everything is impersonal, and as Gangaji says, "Don't ever take anything personally." In this way, no actions can be done to prevent something that has to happen the way it has to happen anyway. But the temptation of idealistic concepts is very great, the temptation of father ideals, of mother ideals, of educational ideals, even of spiritual, educational ideals.

In truth, the child needs neither a "father" nor a "mother" to "educate" it. What do educational concepts signify? They signify the transmission of the mother's or the father's sleeping trance. The child itself is always in connection with the divine Self, and this connection is never interrupted. The child is free. If the child has the tendency to fall asleep, the child has to be given a shake to wake up. The mind cannot be prevented from going through all evolutionary phases, but if the child lives in touch with the Self from the beginning, and not in the mother's and the father's trance of separation, then the child is free. "Father," "mother," and "child" are concepts, limited identifications that arise out of the *thinking mind* but which don't touch reality. The child doesn't identify as "child" by itself. This identification is the result of the false education of the *thinking mind* that identifies with the body and the roles of father and mother.

Normally, children in our society don't grow up with the true teacher. Rather, they grow up with every kind of false teacher possible and this induces the trance. But these false teachers are also instruments of the *one* teacher. The trance happens because it is destined to happen, and there is no "reason" for it. Everything is a process that ultimately, mysteriously, serves realization and awakening.

The simple answer to your question is that there is nothing you can do to fulfill your task as a father because *you* are not the father. There is nothing to do. As long as you believe you are "somebody" who is in control, "somebody" who is in power, there is the idea that you are "somebody" who can do it right or wrong, "somebody" who can fulfill his tasks in the right way or the wrong way. What happens when this idea of doing it right or doing it wrong sinks into stillness? What happens when *you* no longer act, but *it* acts without your knowing how?

I am well aware of the great fears and insecurities that can arise before this moment of letting *it* act. If I believed there was a "somebody" who thought that I should give Darshan, then I also would feel very insecure. But the way it is, Datsang just happens, and there is nothing and nobody to waste a thought about it.

The Self uses these organisms as tools to carry out the play just the way it has to happen. The personal doer is a thought. Outside this thought, there is no personal doer. Find the I-thought, and pursue this I-thought to its apparent source. Find out *who* is the doer, the *real* doer. To say the thought was the driving force behind the action would be the same as to say that electricity was the driving force behind artificial light. But then the question remains, what is the driving force behind electricity, what is the driving force behind the thought? The thought cannot be the true driving force behind the action because there has to be something behind the thought that is driving it. What is the origin of thought? What is the source of thought?

Thought is not the ultimate authority. Experience the mystery that it is actually possible to *be* out of thoughtlessness, out of stillness, and the paradox that everything that happens doesn't actually happen in numbness. Numbness is how the *thinking mind* would interpret its own absence, but on the contrary, everything happens quite amazingly in complete clarity and supreme effectiveness. If uncertainty arises, let it arise, but don't touch it. Uncertainty is just another temptation, which you dive through almost automatically if it is not touched. Uncertainty comes out of fear.

As a parent, the possibility of simply *being* is very exciting, for there is no experience in our Western civilization that shows us the result of a child growing up in an enlightened environment. I once heard Gangaji answer a similar question, and she said that if the parents are free, the child is also free, for in the realization of *yourSelf,* the false trance cannot be transmitted. Transmission, in other words projection, can only happen through thought and an apparent relationship that also happens through thought. If there is no attachment to thoughts, there is no transmission of a trance, because there is nothing to be transmitted, no one to transmit anything, and no one to whom anything is transmitted. There is no child, no father, and no mother.

* * *

It is said that man is in the world to create. Can you say something about creativity?

First of all, who says that?

I'm saying it now.

Well, *I* don't say it.

What do you say then?

I say the only reason you are here is to know who you are. When you know who you are, and when it is expressed in everything, then what do you care about what is happening? Do you see that there are still concepts around wanting to somehow be in control of what should be happening, could be happening, may be happening, or must be happening?

Creativity is not personal, and you need not worry about how something is lived through you. Things you wouldn't have dreamed of may arise, and things you thought would appear don't appear. There is no fixed personality and no fixed qualities manifested through you. Everything manifested through the Self, through consciousness, can change at any time. The personality, as it appears through this organism, at this moment, can change at any time. To believe that there is something that doesn't change is a thought construction. To think, "That's the way I am, that's the way I was, and that's how I know myself" are only thought constructions. It is as if this "personal" edifice of ideas that has a name confirms its existence again and again with the thoughts, "My name is so and so, I am capable of such and such, I am not capable of such and such, etc."

Creativity is the shakti that spontaneously, unpredictably, appears in this moment. It is fresh, without any connection to past, present, or future, although it uses past, present and future. It is without calculation, without control, just like that, with no need of anyone who would have an interest in fitting it into standards of right and wrong.

Okay, but the tricky thing is that when creativity arises, the mind immediately claims and manipulates it — "What will I do with it now? How can it be used?" It is difficult to stay in innocence with it.

When impersonal creativity appears, simply enjoying itself, and there is no one who claims it for him or herself, then in this moment, you touch the quality of true innocence. It is simply the joy of expression, of beauty, and this joy is as impersonal as creativity itself. A problem arises the moment you believe, "*I* am the artist, look what *I* have done!" This is the moment of lost innocence and the joy of expression gets caught once again in the endless loop of the *thinking mind* that tries to use all impersonal qualities to eradicate its own sense of deficiency.

I agree with you, but the mind immediately starts in again with questions of how can I live this.

"You" cannot live this. That's the point, because then the next level of trying to do something immediately appears. It is obviously too simple to be understood by the mind. There is actually, really, nothing to do. Everything simply happens. Actions happen. Creativity happens. Productivity happens. Everything happens by itself, and there is no one who has to integrate this into their life. There is nothing to integrate. Everything simply *is*. If you give up the idea that there is a someone who should live this, it is even simpler. There is nobody who should live anything. Whenever somebody asks me, "Well, how do I integrate this into my everyday life?" I answer with another question, "How do you integrate the ocean into a cup of water?"

When all physical limitation ceases,

in that moment remains what

I AM.

After my accident, I did not have an experience

of not being, but an experience of total, absolute

consciousness. In the moment in which I,

as you would say, woke up, "I" did not wake up,

but images woke up, as if a projector were turned on again

and images were projected onto consciousness.

These images are created by the senses

and are also called "body," "feelings," and "thoughts."

They are images created in consciousness.

In that moment I realized that this world

has no reality. It is simply a dream.

OM (Cedric Parkin), born in 1962, studied psychology and the teachings of the Enneagram. He immersed himself in Sufism and Shamanism and explored the effects of mind-expanding drugs. On August 6, 1990, he had a nearly fatal car accident after which he was clinically dead for two days. This experience was the catalyst for the realization of the true Self, independent of the body and the usual subject/object perceptions. A short time later, he was led to his teacher, Gangaji, and to her teacher, Shri Poonjaji, in Lucknow, India. OM, Gangaji, and Poonjaji all continue the teaching of Non-Duality (Advaita) as it was lived by the great sage, Shri Ramana Maharshi. In regular meetings (Darshans), OM engages in dialogues of Self-inquiry with spiritual seekers in Germany and other European countries.

Glossary

Character Fixation
A term from the teachings of the Enneagram. "Character" means imprinting. Character fixation is an imprinting in time and space, an organized system of subconscious knots within the I-concept (ego).

Darshan
Seeing the Divine. The meeting of the spiritual teacher with his or her students.

Great Self-Inquiry
The investigation into the true nature of man, into what you really are, by using the question, "Who am I?" as taught by Shri Ramana Maharshi.

Karma
Doing, action, activity. Also understood as the chain of cause and effect that results from personally identified actions in time.

Kôan
Japanese. A term from Zen. An enigma given by a (Zen) Master that cannot be solved by the *thinking mind*. The paradoxical nature of the kôan serves to "short-circuit" the logical mind in order to activate deeper layers of the mind, which in turn dissolve in the revelation of truth. In the Zen tradition, there are about 1,700 traditional kôans.

Leela
Divine activities, divine play. The relative. The whole universe is the stage for the Leelas of the divine Self. The play contains the three forces of creation, maintenance, and dissolution.

Mind
Synonym for ego, the body/mind mechanism, also referred to herein as the *thinking mind*. Psyche and intellect are terms that describe only a partial function of a more complex phenomenon.

No-Mind
This term characterizes the apparent contradiction of a mental state in which the *thinking mind* is absent, a "mindless state" of pure intelligence. It describes the natural state of meditation without an I-thought. The *don't-know-mind* is a term used by modern Zen teachers that points to the aspect of innocence that is No-Mind.

Small Self-inquiry
The investigation into the contents of the thinking mind, into that which you are not.

Satsang
Sat means Being, reality, existence, that which does not change. Ultimately, *Sat* is the principle of existence, the basic truth. *Sangha* means group, community, society. Satsang stands for communion with the divine, or with the presence of a saint, sage, or realized person.

Shakti
The divine energy. The basic force of creation, the original expression of which shows in the dynamics between the male and female forces in the human being. Also, Shiva's wife.

Shiva
The third deity in the Hindu-trinity. The God of the
dissolution of everything that is transitory. The destroyer
of ignorance and non-recognition.

Thinking Mind
The mind that is always busy and controls almost
everybody's life, that has created the personal I-structure
and its story of suffering. The mind that functions as the
master.

Working Mind
The mind that is present only when it is needed for the
organization of work. It deals exclusively with the work
that is being done and functions as a servant of the Self.
The "mindless-mind" mind in No-Mind.

GUT SAUNSTORF

ORT DER STILLE

Gut Saunstorf – Place of Stillness is a modern monastery and place for retreat. It is an ideal venue for people seeking a time out for themselves – whether for a few days or longer – for regeneration, reorientation or recovery.

The stylishly restored manor house surrounded by a spacious park is embedded in the hilly landscape south of the Hanseatic city of Wismar. Here the soul finds nourishment, the body relaxes and a space for turning inwards and contemplation unfolds.

Experienced therapists, masseurs as well as our practice for alternative medicine are at your disposal and will be available to support you on request.

Gut Saunstorf – Place of Stillness is home of *several initiatives. At this place* OM C. Parkin is teaching the integral path and a community of disciples is supporting and inspiring the modern monastery.

We offer our guests a program that serves physical and mental healing. The events provided by Gut Saunstorf serve the focused exploration of all aspects of human being. The purpose of *Academy Gut Saunstorf – Place of Stillness* is to bring together the core topics of the inner science.

Be our guest – simply for yourself, in stillness – in this place or at one of our events. Our house is open for you 365 days a year. Here you can stop off and simply be.

Contact information:
Gut Saunstorf - *Place of Stillness*
Gutshaus
23996 Saunstorf, Germany
Email: info@gut-saunstorf.de
www.gut-saunstorf.de

Publisher Contact Information

The publishers of this book invite you to contact the author via
Gut Saunsdorf Retreat Center (see previous page). If you are
interested in further reading along these lines, you may contact
the publisher (contact information follows) or check the website
for current books in the **Consciousness Classics** series:

Gateways Books and Tapes
PO Box 370-BL
Nevada City, CA 95959
(USA)

Email: info@gatewaysbooksandtapes.com
Phone: (530) 271-2239 or (800) 869-0658 (in the U.S.A.)
Website: www.gatewaysbooksandtapes.com

**Gateways Consciousness Classics - A Partial List of Titles
You Can Order**

by Salvatore Brizzi
Draco Daatson's Book: The Never-Asleep Society Revealed
    (translated from the Italian)

by Robert S. de Ropp
The Master Game: Pathways to Higher Consciousness
Self-Completion: Keys to a Meaningful Life
Warrior's Way: A Twentieth Century Odyssey

by Kyle Fite
*Orbit: An Introduction to the Principles and Practices of Bardo-
    Gaming on the Prosperity Path*

by E.J. Gold
Alchemical Sex
American Book of the Dead

The Great Adventure: Talks on Death, Dying and the Bardos
The Human Biological Machine as a Transformational
Apparatus
Parallel Worlds Explored
Practical Work on Self
The Hidden Work
Spiritual Gaming
Tarot Decoded
Visions in the Stone (Intro. by Robert Anton Wilson)

By Barbara Haynes
Every Day a Holy Day: Exercises, Experiments and Practices for
Mindful Living

by Michael Hutchison
The Book of Floating: Exploring the Private Sea

by Ka-Tzetnik 135633
Shivitti: A Vision

by Dr. John C. Lilly
The Deep Self: Consciousness Exploration in the Isolation Tank
The Mind of the Dolphin: A Nonhuman Intelligence
Tanks for the Memories: Floatation Tank Talks (with E.J. Gold)

by Dr. Claudio Naranjo, M.D.
Character & Neurosis: An Integrative View
The Divine Child and the Hero: Inner Meaning in Children's
Literature
The Enneagram of Society: Healing the Soul to Heal the World
The One Quest: A Map of the Ways of Transformation

by Dr. Claude Needham, Ph.D.
The Original Handbook for the Recently Deceased
Just Because Club: Your Metaphysical Fitness Trainer
The Any Game Cookbook: Recipes for Spiritual Gaming

by Mark Olsen
The Golden Buddha Changing Masks: An Opening to
Transformative Theatre

by Kelly Rivera
Journey to the Heart of the Maker